Book of Business Quotations

OTHER ECONOMIST BOOKS

Guide to Analysing Companies
Guide to Business Modelling
Guide to Business Planning
Guide to Cash Management
Guide to Decision-Making
Guide to Economic Indicators
Guide to the European Union
Guide to Financial Management
Guide to Financial Markets
Guide to Hedge Funds
Guide to Investment Strategy
Guide to Management Ideas and Gurus
Guide to Managing Growth
Guide to Organisation Design
Guide to Project Management
Guide to Supply Chain Management
Numbers Guide
Style Guide

Book of Isms
Book of Obituaries
Brands and Branding
Business Consulting
Business Strategy
Buying Professional Services
The City
Coaching and Mentoring
Doing Business in China
Economics
Emerging Markets
Marketing
Megachange
Modern Warfare, Intelligence and Deterrence
Organisation Culture
Successful Strategy Execution
The World of Business

Directors: an A–Z Guide
Economics: an A–Z Guide
Investment: an A–Z Guide
Negotiation: an A–Z Guide

Pocket World in Figures

Book of Business Quotations

Edited by Bill Ridgers

THE ECONOMIST IN ASSOCIATION WITH
PROFILE BOOKS LTD

Published by Profile Books Ltd
3A Exmouth House, Pine Street, London EC1R OJH
www.profilebooks.com

Designed by sue@lambledesign.demon.co.uk
Typeset in EcoType by MacGuru Ltd
info@macguru.org.uk
Printed in Great Britain by Clays, Bungay, Suffolk

A CIP catalogue record for this book is available from the British Library

Hardback ISBN: 978 1 84668 593 4
Ebook ISBN: 978 1 84765 817 3

Contents

About this book / xii
Introduction / xiii

A Accountants and accountancy / 1
Advertising / 3
Advice / 6
Agriculture business / 9
The airline industry / 9
Ambition / 10
America / 12
Appraisals / 14
The arts / 15

B Banks and bankers / 18
Bills / 20
The board / 21
The boss / 22
Branding / 23
Bureaucracy / 24
Business education / 26
Business entertaining / 27
Business travel / 28

C Capitalism / 29
The car industry / 32
Change / 33
Civility / 36
Joking aside: five quotes from comedians / 37
Committees / 38
Communication / 38
Communism and socialism / 39
Competition / 40
Complacency / 43
Conferences / 43
Conflict and the arms industry / 44
Consultants and consulting / 45
Consumerism / 46
Corporations / 49
Costs / 50
Creativity / 51
Credit / 54
Crime / 55
Culture / 55
Customers and customer service / 56
Cynicism / 60

D Data, information and statistics / 61
Debt / 63
Decision-making / 64
Delegation / 66
Design / 66
Development / 67
Discipline / 68

Dishonesty / 68
Diversity / 69
Downturns and economic turmoil / 70
The drugs industry / 70

E Economics / 72
In brief: five epigrams / 74
Education / 76
Egotism / 76
Emerging markets / 77
Entrepreneurs and entrepreneurialism / 77
The environment / 80
Envy and jealousy / 81
Ethics / 82
Europe / 85
Experience / 86
Expertise / 87

F Failure / 89
Showing character: five quotes from film
    and TV / 91
Family business / 92
The film industry / 93
Financial crises / 93
Following the herd / 94
Foot-in-mouth and blunt honesty / 95
Friendship / 96
Fulfilment / 97
Fun / 97

G   Gambling / 99
Globalisation / 99
Greed / 101
Growth / 102

H   Happiness / 104
Hard work / 105
Hiring / 108
Honesty / 109
Hubris / 111

I   Innovation / 112
Insurance / 118
The internet / 118
Intuition / 119
Investing / 120

K   Knowledge / 124
Knowledge workers / 125

L   Labour / 127
Novel thoughts: five quotes from
    literature / 130
Lawyers and the law / 131
Laziness / 133
Leadership / 135
Luck / 138

M Management speak and jargon / 140
Management thinking / 142
Managers and management / 142
Words from the wise: five quotes from
    management gurus / 143
Manufacturing / 147
Market research / 147
Marketing / 148
Markets / 151
The media / 152
Meetings / 154
Mergers, demergers and acquisitions / 155
Money / 156
Motivation / 159
The music industry / 160

N Negotiation and dealmaking / 162

O Obsession / 163
Obstacles / 163
Office life / 164
The oil and gas industry / 166
The oldest profession / 168
Operations / 169
Optimism / 170

P Performance / 171
Philanthropy / 171
Philosophy / 172

Planning / 172
Poverty / 173
Power / 174
Predictions / 175
Price / 175
Procrastination / 176
Products / 177
The despatch box: five quotes from
    politicians / 178
Progress / 179
Promotion / 180
Purpose / 181

R   Regulation / 182
Remuneration / 183
Reputation / 185
Responsibility / 186
Retirement / 186
Risk / 187

S   The sack / 189
Science / 190
Secretaries / 190
Self-employment / 191
Self-interest / 191
Selling / 192
Show business / 193
Small and medium-sized businesses / 194

Sport / 194
Start-ups / 195
Strategy / 196
Success / 200
Supply chains / 204

T Talent / 205
Taxes / 207
Teamwork / 208
Technology / 210
The tobacco industry / 214
Training / 214

U Unemployment / 215
Unions and industrial relations / 216

V Value / 219

W Wealth / 221
Women in business / 225
Work-life balance / 227

Acknowledgements / 229
Index / 230

About this book

This book is not meant to represent an exhaustive list of business quotations. Rather it is a collection of quotations that the editor believes to be particularly pertinent, witty and enjoyable. Where possible they have been taken from the original source and this has been noted in the text. Some quotations have been widely attributed to their author but the original source could not be found; these have been left without sources. In rare cases where there is a reasonable chance that the quotation is apocryphal, this has been noted in the text as "attributed".

Introduction

From the day that humans first learned to write, they have written about business. When archaeologists discovered Sumerian tablets dating from the 4th millennium BC, considered to be the first examples of the written word, they uncovered not musings on love, family or war, but a record of trade. No sooner had writing developed to encompass abstract thought than man was aphorising on the vagaries of commerce. "Choose a job you love and you will never have to work a day in your life," wrote Confucius, a Chinese philosopher, in 500BC. It is a trend that has continued ever since. Two-and-a-half-thousand years later, a philosopher for a different age, Homer Simpson, was telling his colleagues at a nuclear power plant: "If you don't like your job you don't strike. You just go in every day and do it really half-assed. That's the American way."

Why do we find business quotations so compelling? There are several reasons. The first is aesthetic. In a world often thought of as cold and calculating, there is art to be found the pithy quotation that encapsulates a deeper truth, as the quotes from Confucius and Homer demonstrate. Even better if it is plain funny: "If I was as rich as Rockefeller," said Ronnie Barker, a British comedian, "I'd be richer than

Rockefeller, because I'd do a bit of window cleaning on the side."

Then there is reflection, writing about business as an academic pursuit. From Francis Bacon to Karl Marx to Thomas Friedman, it is a noble tradition. Is there a better definition of capitalism than Joseph Schumpeter's phrase "creative destruction"? Has anyone understood the role of the company better than Peter Drucker, when he said that "there is only one definition of business purpose: to create a customer"?

But we also have a desire to learn from the success of others. We think we can distil the philosophy of Warren Buffett, Henry Ford or Jack Welch in just a few of their well-chosen words. If we condense everything that made Steve Jobs great, we are left with just one simple sentence: "Simple can be harder than complex: you have to work hard to get your thinking clean to make it simple."

Lastly, if we are honest, we read business quotations because we love a cutting comment – and a good moan. Most of us will have to endure the drudgery of work, and it makes us feel better that we are not alone. "When you grow up you'll be put in a container called a cubicle. The bleak oppressiveness will warp your spine and destroy your capacity to feel joy. Luckily you'll have a boss like me to motivate you with something called fear." So said Dilbert, a character in a comic strip, who can speak to our souls.

Nostalgia ain't what it used to be

Given that 6,000 years have passed since that
trailblazing Mesopotamian first picked up a stylus
and etched his labour costs into a rock, we might ask
whether the golden age of the business quotation
has now passed. Businessmen, in general, have
become more anodyne. The quotation hunter, you
might imagine, pines for the heady days of the "Mad
Men". If we are to believe the glitzy drama, this was
a time when an executive's day was spent guzzling
Scotch and, it seemed, spouting one memorable line
after another. But, in fact, the businessmen of the
1950s and 1960s have left us with surprisingly few
zingers. (Perhaps they were just too drunk to
remember all the clever lines they came out with.)

A Scotch before noon is now frowned upon in most
businesses. Much of the business world bows to
24-hour news and public-relations despots, who
strangle interesting statements at birth for fear of
causing offence and a slide in the share price. This
has led to a depressing escalation in euphemism and
management speak: the art of sounding as if you are
saying something when you are not. "Negative
growth", explains the PR director, sounds more
impressive than "loss"; "rationalisation" is more
intellectually defensible than "job cuts".

But business has not really changed. There are still
plenty of places where you can find shoot-from-the-
hip chief executives. Indeed, today may well be the

quotation's golden age. Silicon Valley has given us the wisdom of Steve Jobs and Jeff Bezos. Airlines still throw up loud-mouthed executives such as Michael O'Leary and Herb Kelleher. And the normally strait-laced world of investment has given us perhaps the most quotable businessman of our age, Warren Buffett. The sage of Omaha recently wrote in a letter to his shareholders:

> In a bull market, one must avoid the error of the preening duck that quacks boastfully after a torrential rainstorm, thinking that its paddling skills have caused it to rise in the world. A right-thinking duck would instead compare its position after the downpour to that of the other ducks on the pond.

It is at once pithy and reflective, and says much about why he is so successful. And, of course, it is a delightfully cutting swipe at those masters of the universe who bestride Wall Street. In other words, it is perhaps the perfect quotation.

A

❝ Accountants and accountancy

When you make a mistake of adding the date to the right side of the accounting statement, you must add it to the left side too.

Anon

The term "earnings" has a precise ring to it. And when an earnings figure is accompanied by an unqualified auditor's certificate, a naive reader might think it comparable in certitude to pi, calculated to dozens of decimal places. In reality, however, earnings can be as pliable as putty when a charlatan heads the company reporting them.

Warren Buffett, investor (1930–), letter to shareholders of Berkshire Hathaway

Mr Anchovy, but you see your report here says that you are an extremely dull person. You see, our experts describe you as an appallingly dull fellow, unimaginative, timid, lacking in initiative, spineless, easily dominated, no sense of humour, tedious company and irrepressibly drab and awful. And whereas in most professions these would be considerable drawbacks, in chartered accountancy they are a positive boon.

John Cleese, comedian (1939–), "Vocational Guidance Counsellor", *Monty Python* sketch (British TV series, 1969)

An accountant applied for a job. The interviewer asked him, "How much is two and two?" The accountant got up from his chair, went over to the door and closed it then came back and sat down. He leaned across the desk and said in a low voice, "How much do you want it to be?"

Joke

Budget: a mathematical confirmation of your suspicions.

A.A. Latimer, author

Accounting and control – that is mainly what is needed for the "smooth working", for the proper functioning, of the first phase of communist society.

Vladimir Lenin (1870–1924), *The State and Revolution* (1917)

There's no business like show business, but there are several businesses like accounting.

David Letterman, chat-show host (1947–)

I have no use for bodyguards, but I have very specific use for two highly trained certified public accountants.

Elvis Presley, musician (1935–77)

Balanced budget requirements seem more likely to produce accounting ingenuity than genuinely balanced budgets.

Thomas Sowell, economist (1930–)

66 Advertising

Let me try and clarify some of this for you. Best Company Supermarkets are not interested in selling wholesome foods. They are not worried about the nation's health. What is concerning them, is that the nation appears to be getting worried about its health, and that is what's worrying Best Co, because Best Co wants to go on selling them what it always has, ie white breads, baked beans, canned foods, and that suppurating, fat-squirting little heart attack traditionally known as the British sausage.

Denis Dimbleby Bagley, character in *How to Get Ahead in Advertising* (feature film, 1989)

Without promotion something terrible happens ... Nothing!

P.T. Barnum, showman (1810–91)

Doing business without advertising is like winking at a girl in the dark.

Stuart Henderson Britt, academic (1907–79), *New York Herald Tribune*, October 1956

Make it simple. Make it memorable. Make it inviting to look at. Make it fun to read.

Leo Burnett, advertising executive (1891–1971)

Any fool can write a bad ad, but it takes a real genius to keep his hands off a good one.

Leo Burnett

Fun without sell gets nowhere, but sell without fun tends to become obnoxious.

Leo Burnett

There was a time when I used to get lots of ideas ... I thought up the Seven Deadly Sins in one afternoon. The only thing I've come up with recently is advertising.

Peter Cook, satirist (1937–95), as the devil in *Bedazzled* (feature film, 1967)

If you don't like what's being said, change the conversation.

Donald Draper, character in *Mad Men* (American TV series)

Advertisements contain the only truths to be relied on in a newspaper.

Thomas Jefferson, American president (1743–1826), letter to Nathaniel Macon

Advertising may be described as the science of arresting the human intelligence long enough to get money from it.

Stephen Leacock, writer (1869–1944), *The Garden of Folly* (2004)

Advertising is the greatest art form of the 20th century.

Marshall McLuhan, teacher and philosopher (1911–80), *Advertising Age*, 1976

The business of the advertiser is to see that we go about our business with some magic spell or tune or slogan throbbing quietly in the background of our minds.

Marshall McLuhan, *Commonweal*, September 1953

The modern Little Red Riding Hood, reared on singing commercials, has no objection to being eaten by the wolf.

Marshall McLuhan, philosopher (1911–80), "Book of the Hour", *The Mechanical Bride* (1951)

The medium is the message.

Marshall McLuhan, *The Medium is the Massage: An Inventory of Effects* (1967)

Never write an advertisement which you wouldn't want your own family to read. You wouldn't tell lies to your own wife. Don't tell them to mine. Do as you would be done by. If you tell lies about a product, you will be found out – either by the Government, which will prosecute you, or by the consumer, who will punish you by not buying your product a second time. Good products can be sold by honest advertising. If you don't think the product is good, you have no business to be advertising it.

David Ogilvy, advertising executive (1911–99) *Confessions of an Advertising Man* (1961)

The public are swine; advertising is the rattling of a stick inside a swill-bucket.

George Orwell, author (1903–50), *Keep the Aspidistra Flying* (1936)

In our factory, we make lipstick. In our advertising, we sell hope.

Charles Revson, founder of Revlon (1906–95)

Half the money I spend on advertising is wasted; the trouble is I don't know which half.

John Wanamaker, merchant (1838–1922), attributed

Advertising is legalised lying.

H.G. Wells, author (1866–1946)

❝ Advice

The first thing a new employee should do on the job is learn to recognise his boss's voice on the phone.

Martin Buxbaum, author and humorist (1912–)

The only unforgivable sin in business is to run out of cash.

Harold Geneen, businessman, (1910–97)

Never ascribe to malice that which can be explained by incompetence.

Robert J. Hanlon, *Hanlon's razor* (1980) (sometimes attributed to Napoleon Bonaparte)

The main thing to remember is, the main thing is the main thing.

Brigadier General Gary E. Huffman

Simple can be harder than complex: you have to work hard to get your thinking clean to make it simple. But it's worth it in the end because once you get there, you can move mountains.

Steve Jobs, founder of Apple (1955–2011), quoted in *BusinessWeek*, May 1998

Ten minutes are not just one-sixth of your hourly pay. Ten minutes are a piece of yourself. Divide your life into ten-minute units and sacrifice as few of them as possible in meaningless activity

Ingvar Kamprad, founder of IKEA (1926–)

Never pick up someone else's ringing phone.

Mark McCormack, writer (1930–2003), *What You'll Never Learn on the Internet* (2001)

Don't worry about your physical shortcomings. I am no Greek god. Don't get too much sleep and don't tell anybody your troubles. Appearances count: get a sun lamp to keep you looking as though you have just come back from somewhere expensive; maintain an elegant address even if you have to live in the attic. Never nickel when short of cash. Borrow big, but always repay promptly.

Aristotle Onassis, shipping magnate (1906–75)

If you're not confused, you're not paying attention.

Tom Peters, management writer (1942–)

I want to share something with you: the three little sentences that will get you through life. Number 1: Cover for me. Number 2: Oh, good idea, boss! Number 3: It was like that when I got here.

Homer Simpson, character in *The Simpsons* (American TV series)

Son, you be sure to set your goals so high you can't possibly accomplish them in one lifetime ... I made the mistake of setting my goals too low and now I'm having a hard time coming up with new ones

Robert Turner, father of Ted Turner, media mogul

Swim upstream. Go the other way. Ignore the conventional wisdom.

Sam Walton, founder of Walmart (1918–82)

66 Agriculture business

He who works his land will have abundant food, but he who chases fantasies lacks judgment.
The Bible, Proverbs 12:11

Agriculture is now a motorised food industry, the same thing in its essence as the production of corpses in the gas chambers and the extermination camps, the same thing as blockades and the reduction of countries to famine, the same thing as the manufacture of hydrogen bombs.
Martin Heidegger, philosopher (1889–1976), lecture, 1949

When you concentrate on agriculture and industry and are frugal in expenditures, Heaven cannot impoverish your state.
Xun Zi, Confucian philosopher (312–230BC)

66 The airline industry

If the Wright brothers were alive today Wilbur would have to fire Orville to reduce costs.
Herb Kelleher, founder of Southwest Airlines (1931–), quoted in *USA Today*, June 1994

We need a recession. We have had ten years of growth. A recession gets rid of crappy loss-making

airlines and it means we can buy aircraft more cheaply.
Michael O'Leary, CEO of Ryanair (1961–), quoted in the *Daily Telegraph*, November 2008

If we went into the funeral business, people would stop dying.
Martin Shugrue, PanAm executive (1941–99)

A recession is when you have to tighten your belt; depression is when you have no belt to tighten. When you've lost your trousers – you're in the airline business.
Adam Thomson, former chairman of British Caledonian (1926–2000)

In one fell swoop, we have shrunken the earth.
Juan Tripp, founder of PanAm (1899–1981), on the introduction of the first jet-engine planes

Running an airline is like having a baby: fun to conceive, but hell to deliver.
C.E. Woolman (1889–1966), founder of Delta Air Lines

Ambition

Ambition is a poor excuse for not having sense enough to be lazy.
Edgar Bergen, ventriloquist (1903–78)

[Ambitious men] may not cease, but as a dog in a wheel, a bird in a cage, or a squirrel in a chain, so Budaeus compares them; they climb and climb still, with much labour, but never make an end, never at the top.

Robert Burton, scholar (1577–1640), *The Anatomy of Melancholy* (1621)

The great Western Disease lies in the phrase, "I will be happy when ..."

Marshall Goldsmith, management writer (1949–), "Making a Resolution that Matters", *Fast Company*, February 2004

The worst fault of the working classes is telling their children they're not going to succeed, saying: "There is life, but it's not for you."

John Mortimer, barrister (1923–2009)

Empty pockets never held anyone back. Only empty heads and empty hearts can do that.

Norman Vincent Peale, church minister (1898–1993), *Enthusiasm Makes a Difference* (1967)

Ambition is a dream with a V8 engine.

Elvis Presley, musician (1935–77)

Why should we be in such desperate haste to succeed and in such desperate enterprises? If a man does not keep pace with his companions, perhaps it is because he hears a different drummer. Let him

step to the music which he hears, however measured
or far away.

Henry David Thoreau, author (1817–1862), *Walden* (1854)

❝ America

The chief business of the American people is
business.

Calvin Coolidge, American president (1872–1933), address to
the American Society of Newspaper Editors

I was slightly cynical of the American mentality
before I came over here, but now I preach it. Here, no
one's going to tear you down if you buy yourself a
$300,000 car. They're likely to say: "Well, you
probably worked hard for it. Good luck to you."

Simon Cowell, showbusiness man (1959–), quoted in the *New
York Times*, May 2004

If you were really, really, really rich ... what part of
your life would be American? If you had the money,
I'd bet you'd drive a German car, wear British shoes
and an Italian suit, keep your savings in a Swiss
bank, vacation in Koh Samui with shopping
expeditions to Cannes, fly Emirates, develop a palate
for South African wine, hire a French-trained chef,
buy a few dozen Indian and Chinese companies, and
pay Dubai-style taxes. Were you to have the
untrammelled economic freedom to, I'd bet you'd
run screaming from big, fat, wheezing American

business as usual, and its coterie of lacklustre, slightly bizarre, and occasionally grody "innovations": spray cheese, ATM fees, designer diapers, disposable lowest-common-denominator junk made by prison labour, Muzak-filled big-box stores, five thousand channels and nothing on but endless reruns of "Toddlers in Tiaras".

Umair Haque, consultant, *Harvard Business Review*, October 2011

Americans are apt to be unduly interested in discovering what average opinion believes average opinion to be; and this national weakness finds its nemesis in the stock market.

John Maynard Keynes, economist (1883–1946), *The General Theory of Employment Interest and Money* (1936)

The problem with American management today is that it has succeeded in assuming many of the appearances and privileges of professionalism while evading the attendant constraints and responsibilities.

Rakesh Khurana, Nitin Nohria and **Daniel Penrice**, *HBS Working Knowledge*, February 2005

Businessmen are the one group that distinguishes capitalism and the American way of life from the totalitarian statism that is swallowing the rest of the world. All the other social groups – workers, farmers, professional men, scientists, soldiers – exist under dictatorships, even though they exist in chains, in terror, in misery, and in progressive self-destruction. But there is no such group as businessmen under a dictatorship. Their place is taken by armed thugs: by bureaucrats and commissars. Businessmen are the symbol of a free society – the symbol of America.

Ayn Rand, author (1905–82), *Capitalism: The Unknown Ideal* (1966)

Americans used to be "citizens." Now we are "consumers."

Vicki Robin, writer (1945–), *Your Money or Your Life* (1999)

What's great about this country is America started the tradition where the richest consumers buy essentially the same things as the poorest. You can be watching TV and see Coca-Cola, and you can know that the President drinks Coke, Liz Taylor drinks Coke, and just think, you can drink Coke, too. A Coke is a Coke and no amount of money can get you a better Coke than the one the bum on the corner is drinking. All the Cokes are the same and all the Cokes are good.

Andy Warhol, artist (1928–87)

6 Appraisals

An appraisal is where you have an exchange of opinion with your boss. It's called an exchange of opinion because you go in with your opinion and leave with their opinion.

Guy Browning, humorist (1964–), *Office Politics: How Work Really Works* (2006)

66 The arts

The culture industry not so much adapts to the reactions of its customers as it counterfeits them.

Theodor Adorno, sociologist (1903–69)

Charge less, but charge. Otherwise, you will not be taken seriously, and you do your fellow artists no favours if you undercut the market.

Elizabeth Aston, author, *The True Darcy Spirit* (2006)

I'm not a driven businessman, but a driven artist. I never think about money. Beautiful things make money.

Geoffrey Beene, fashion designer (1924–2004)

I find it rather easy to portray a businessman. Being bland, rather cruel and incompetent comes naturally to me.

John Cleese, comedian (1939–)

I can't change the fact that my paintings don't sell. But the time will come when people will recognise that they are worth more than the value of the paints used in the picture.

Vincent van Gogh, artist (1853–90)

Being good in business is the most fascinating kind of art. Making money is art and working is art and good business is the best art.

Andy Warhol, artist (1928–87)

B

66 Banks and bankers

I am just a banker "doing God's work".

Lloyd Blankfein, CEO of Goldman Sachs (1954–), quoted in
the *Wall Street Journal*, May 2010

Banks are the temples of America. This is a holy war.
Our economy is our religion.

Giannina Braschi, novelist (1953–), *United States of Banana*
(2011)

Mr Victim, I'm glad to say that I've got the go-ahead
to lend you the money you require. Yes, of course we
will want as security the deeds of your house, of
your aunt's house, of your second cousin's house, of
your wife's parents' house, and of your grannie's
bungalow, and we will in addition need a controlling
interest in your new company, unrestricted access to
your private bank account, the deposit in our vaults
of your three children as hostages and a full legal
indemnity against any acts of embezzlement carried
out against you by any members of our staff during
the normal course of their duties ... no, I'm afraid we
couldn't accept your dog instead of your youngest

child, we would like to suggest a brand new scheme of ours under which 51% of both your dog and your wife pass to us in the event of your suffering a serious accident.

John Cleese, comedian (1939–), "Merchant Banker", *Monty Python* sketch (British TV series, 1969)

Perhaps it is one secret of their power that, having studied the fluctuations of prices, they know that history is inflationary, and that money is the last thing a wise man will hoard.

Will Durant, writer (1885–1961), *The Lessons of History* (1986)

The process by which banks create money is so simple that the mind is repelled.

John Kenneth Galbraith, economist (1908–2006), *Money: Whence It Came, Where It Went* (1975)

The chronic problem in the City is institutionalised dishonesty, people behaving with as much integrity as is possible but having to live in an environment which puts the firms' interests before those of the customer, and seeks on a daily basis to separate the customer from as much of his money as it can get away with. Today's problem is honest people in dishonest firms.

Anthony Hilton, writer, *Evening Standard*, October 2011

The art and mystery of banks ... is established on the principle that "private debts are a public blessing".

That the evidences of those private debts, called bank notes, become active capital, and aliment the whole commerce, manufactures, and agriculture of the United States. Here are a set of people, for instance, who have bestowed on us the great blessing of running in our debt about two hundred millions of dollars, without our knowing who they are, where they are, or what property they have to pay this debt when called on; nay, who have made us so sensible of the blessings of letting them run in our debt, that we have exempted them by law from the repayment of these debts beyond a given proportion (generally estimated at one-third). And to fill up the measure of blessing, instead of paying, they receive an interest on what they owe from those to whom they owe; for all the notes, or evidences of what they owe, which we see in circulation, have been lent to somebody on an interest which is levied again on us through the medium of commerce. And they are so ready still to deal out their liberalities to us, that they are now willing to let themselves run in our debt ninety millions more, on our paying them the same premium of six or eight per cent interest, and on the same legal exemption from the repayment of more than thirty millions of the debt, when it shall be called for.

Thomas Jefferson, American president (1743–1826), letter to John W. Eppes

Banking establishments are more dangerous than standing armies, and that the principle of spending money to be paid by posterity under the name of funding is but swindling futurity on a large scale.

Thomas Jefferson, letter to John Taylor

The old saying holds. Owe your banker £1,000 and you are at his mercy; owe him £1m and the position is reversed.

John Maynard Keynes, economist (1883–1946), *Treasury Papers* (1945)

The men on the trading floor may not have been to school, but they have PhDs in man's ignorance.

Michael Lewis, author (1960–), *The Big Short* (2010)

One rule which woe betides the banker who fails to
    heed it
Never lend any money to anybody unless they don't
    need it.

Ogden Nash, poet (1902–71), *The Face is Familiar*

Let me issue and control a nation's money and I care not who writes the laws.

Mayer Amschel Rothschild, banker (1744–1812)

Bankers – pillars of society who are going to hell if there is a God and He has been accurately quoted.

John Ralston Saul, aphorist (1947–), *The Doubter's Companion: A Dictionary of Aggressive Common Sense* (1994)

The faults of the burglar are the qualities of the financier: the manners and habits of a duke would cost a city clerk his situation.

George Bernard Shaw, playwright (1856–1950), *Major Barbara*

The modern banking process manufactures currency out of nothing. The process is perhaps the most astounding piece of sleight of hand that was ever invented ... If you want to be slaves of the bankers, and pay the cost of your own slavery, then let the banks create currency.

Josiah Stemp, former governor of the Bank of England (1880–1941), address at the University of Texas, 1927

66 Bills

There's always something to be thankful for. If you can't pay your bills, you can be thankful you're not one of your creditors.

Anon

Bills, bills, bills. One is born, one runs up bills, one dies ... Sometimes I feel like a pelican: whichever way I turn, I've still got an enormous bill in front of me.

Edmund Blackadder, character in *Blackadder the Third* (British TV series, 1987)

Song, dance, wine, music, stories from the Persian,
All pretty pastimes in which no offence is;

But Lambro saw all these things with aversion,
Perceiving in his absence such expenses,
Dreading the climax of all human ills,
The inflammation of his weekly bills.

Lord Byron, poet (1788–1824), *Don Juan*

A bill, by the bye, is the most extraordinary locomotive engine that the genius of man ever produced. It would keep on running during the longest lifetime, without ever once stopping of its own accord.

Charles Dickens, novelist (1812–70), *Pickwick Papers* (1836–37)

It is only by not paying one's bills that one can hope to live in the memory of the commercial classes.

Oscar Wilde, writer (1854–1900)

❝ The board

Too many people are on boards because they want to have nice-looking visiting cards.

Utz Frecht, quoted in the *Sunday Times*, October 2000

Directors are generally disastrous in their effect on young managements. If not firmly under the thumb of the chief executive, they indulge a nervous impulse: they keep pulling up the flowers to see how the roots are growing.

Robert Townsend, businessman and author (1920–98), *Up the Organization* (1970)

You never ask board members what they think. You tell them what you're going to do.

Bill Watkins, businessman (1953–), *Fortune*, November 2006

I just don't like quotas in the boardroom or in the office. Winning companies are meritocracies. They practice differentiation, making a clear distinction between top, middle and bottom performers. This system is candid and fair, and it's the most effective way for an organisation to field the best team.

Jack Welch, businessman (1935–), *Winning: The Ultimate Business How-To Book* (2005)

❝ The boss

If you think your boss is stupid, remember: you wouldn't have a job if he was any smarter.

John Gotti, gangster (1940–2002)

The only time some people work like a horse is when the boss rides them.

Gabriel Heatter, broadcaster (1890–1972)

It takes nerves of steel to stay neurotic.

Herb Kelleher, founder of Southwest Airlines (1931–)

Hierarchy is the company that has its face to the CEO and its ass to the customer.

Jonas Ridderstrale and **Kjell Nordstrom**, *Funky Business* (2001)

People ask the difference between a leader and a boss. The leader works in the open and the boss in covert. The leader leads and the boss drives.

Theodore Roosevelt, American president (1858–1919)

Wise bosses are devoted to knowing what they don't know. They act boldly on facts they have right now, but search for signs they are wrong – seeking a healthy balance between courage and humility.

Robert Sutton, academic, *Good Boss, Bad Boss* (2010)

Branding

If the name "Starbucks" is so strongly associated with coffee that you have to remove the name in order to launch another product, does that not suggest that the corporate strategy is out of synch with customer understanding?

Nigel Hollis, writer (1958–), *Harvard Business Review*, January 2011

A brand is not a product or a promise or a feeling. It's the sum of all the experiences you have with a company.

Amir Kassaei, advertising executive (1968–)

A product is something made in a factory; a brand is something that is bought by the customer. A product can be copied by a competitor; a brand is unique. A product can be quickly outdated; a successful brand is timeless.

Stephen King, advertising executive (1931–2006)

If you are not a brand, you are a commodity.

Philip Kotler, academic (1931–)

The most powerful concept in marketing is owning a word in the prospect's mind.

Al Ries and **Jack Trout,** *The 22 Immutable Laws Of Marketing* (1994)

If you can get your customers to prefer your product or service on the basis of more than just the product or service itself, you've got it made.

Sergio Zymen, marketing executive (1945–), *The End of Marketing as We Know It* (1999)

66 Bureaucracy

The purpose of bureaucracy is to compensate for incompetence and lack of discipline – a problem that largely goes away if you have the right people in the first place.

Jim Collins, management writer (1958–), *Good to Great* (2001)

Hell hath no fury like a bureaucrat scorned.

Milton Friedman, economist (1912–2006), *Newsweek,* December 1975

Simple, clear purpose and principles give rise to complex and intelligent behaviour. Complex rules and regulations give rise to simple and stupid behaviour.

Dee Hock, businessman (1929–)

Bureaucracy defends the status quo long past the time when the quo has lost its status.

Laurence Peter, teacher and writer (1919–90)

Bureaucratic administration means fundamentally the exercise of control on the basis of knowledge.

Max Weber, sociologist (1864–1920), *The Theory of Social and Economic Organization* (1968)

I don't give a damn if we get a little bureaucracy as long as we get the results. If it bothers you, yell at it. Kick it. Scream at it. Break it!

Jack Welch, businessman (1935–), *BusinessWeek*, June 1998

We are not hapless beings caught in the grip of forces we can do little about, and wholesale damnations of our society only lend a further mystique to organisation. Organisation has been made by man; it can be changed by man.

William Whyte, writer (1917–99), *The Organization Man* (1956)

It is not necessary to imagine the world ending in fire or ice. There are two other possibilities: one is paper work and the other is nostalgia.

Frank Zappa, musician (1940–93)

66 Business education

"Whom are you?" he asked, for he had attended business college.

George Ade, writer (1866–1944), *The Steel Box* (1898)

In college, Yuppies major in business administration. If to meet certain requirements they have to take a liberal arts course, they take Business Poetry.

Dave Barry, writer (1947–)

The mark of a true MBA is that he is often wrong but seldom in doubt.

Robert Buzzell, academic (1933–2004)

Learning is not doing; it is reflecting on doing.

Henry Mintzberg, academic (1939–), *Managers not MBAs* (2004)

Trying to teach management to someone who has never managed is like trying to teach psychology to someone who has never met another human being.

Henry Mintzberg, *Managers not MBAs* (2004)

Cognitive learning no more makes a manager than it does a swimmer. The latter will drown the first time he jumps into the water if his coach never takes him out of the lecture hall, gets him wet and gives him feedback on his performance.

Henry Mintzberg, "The Managers Job: Folklore and Fact", *Harvard Business Review*, July–August 1975

To borrow from Warren Buffett, don't ask the barber if you need a haircut – and don't ask an academic if what he does is relevant.

Nassim Nicholas Taleb, writer (1960–), *The Black Swan: The Impact of the Highly Improbable* (2007)

66 Business entertaining

Sire, in eight words I will reveal to you all the wisdom that I have distilled through all these years from all the writings of all the economists who once practised their science in your kingdom. Here is my text: "There ain't no such thing as free lunch."

Anon business fable

The quality of food is in inverse proportion to a dining room's altitude, especially atop bank and hotel buildings (airplanes are an extreme example).

Bryan Miller, restaurant critic

[A] piece of advice I'll give junior writers; when you get to the point where they take you to lunch, let the editor suggest where to go.

Jerry Pournelle, writer (1933–)

I approve of the dining system; it puts people in good humour, and makes them agree when they otherwise might not: a dinner lubricates business.

William Stowell, judge (1745–1836), quoted in *Life of Lord Stowell* by William Townsend (1845)

" Business travel

There are only two reasons to sit in the back row of an airplane: Either you have diarrhoea, or you're anxious to meet people who do.

Henry Kissinger, diplomat (1923–)

No one travelling on a business trip would be missed if he failed to arrive.

Thorstein Veblen, economist (1857–1929)

C

❝ Capitalism

Capitalism is the legitimate racket of the ruling class.

Al Capone, gangster (1899–1947)

Some people regard private enterprise as a predatory tiger to be shot. Others look on it as a cow they can milk. Not enough people see it as a healthy horse, pulling a sturdy wagon.

Winston Churchill, British prime minister (1874–1965)

The historical debate is over. The answer is free-market capitalism.

Thomas Friedman, writer (1953–), *The Lexus and the Olive Tree: Understanding Globalization* (1999)

It is probably true that business corrupts everything it touches. It corrupts politics, sports, literature, art, labour unions and so on. But business also corrupts and undermines monolithic totalitarianism. Capitalism is at its liberating best in a non-capitalist environment.

Eric Hoffer, philosopher (1902–83), *New York Times*, April 1971

If the Treasury were to fill old bottles with banknotes, bury them at suitable depths in disused coal mines which are then filled up to the surface with town rubbish, and leave it to private enterprise on well tried principles of laissez-faire to dig the notes up again (the right to do so being obtained, of course, by tendering for leases of the note-bearing territory), there need be no more unemployment and, with the help of the repercussions, the real income of the community, and its capital wealth also, would probably become a good deal greater than it actually is.

John Maynard Keynes, economist (1883–1946), *The General Theory of Employment Interest and Money* (1936)

Capitalism is the astounding belief that the most wickedest of men will do the most wickedest of things for the greatest good of everyone.

John Maynard Keynes

What we have been living for three decades is frontier capitalism, with the frontier constantly shifting location from crisis to crisis, moving on as soon as the law catches up.

Naomi Klein, author (1970–), *The Shock Doctrine: The Rise of Disaster Capitalism* (2007)

Capital is money, capital is commodities. By virtue of it being value, it has acquired the occult ability to add value to itself. It brings forth live offspring, or, at least, lays golden eggs.

Karl Marx, philosopher (1818–83), *Das Kapital* (1867)

Capitalism is being killed by its achievements.

Joseph Schumpeter, economist (1883–1950), *Capitalism, Socialism and Democracy* (1942)

The opening up of new markets, foreign or domestic, and the organisational development from the craft shop and factory to such concerns as US Steel illustrate the same process of industrial mutation – if I may use that biological term – that incessantly revolutionises the economic structure from within, incessantly destroying the old one, incessantly creating a new one. This process of Creative Destruction is the essential fact about capitalism.

Joseph Schumpeter, *Capitalism, Socialism and Democracy* (1942)

The capitalist is merely a man who does not spend all that is earned by work.

Samuel Smiles, author (1812–1904), *Thrift* (1875)

Capitalism knows only one colour: that colour is green; all else is necessarily subservient to it, hence, race, gender and ethnicity cannot be considered within it.

Thomas Sowell, economist (1930–)

To become rich is glorious.

Deng Xiaoping, Chinese Communist Party leader (1904–77)

❝ The car industry

Car designers are just going to have to come up with an automobile that outlasts the payments.

Erma Bombeck, humorist (1927–96)

As long as the unwritten rule stands that the best way to achieve success at GM is to be a good finance man, the bad habit of juggling numbers in order to present the picture people want to see cannot be broken.

Maryann Keller, analyst, *Rude Awakening: The Rise, Fall, and Struggle for Recovery of General Motors* (1989)

The reason American cars don't sell anymore is that they have forgotten how to design the American Dream. What does it matter if you buy a car today or six months from now, because cars are not beautiful. That's why the American auto industry is in trouble: no design, no desire.

Karl Lagerfeld, fashion designer (1933–)

For too many years, Detroit companies' primary tactic for fighting back has been to shift consumers' attention to the future, while leveraging their past as

a sentimental weapon that they have used to
obscure the deficiencies of the present.

Micheline Maynard, writer, *The End of Detroit* (2003)

General Motors, with its huge credit, financing and
mortgage operations, is less of a car company than a
bank that builds cars.

Micheline Maynard, *The End of Detroit* (2003)

Revitalising General Motors is like teaching an
elephant to tap dance. You find the sensitive spot and
start poking.

Ross Perot, businessman and American presidential candidate
(1930–), *International Management*, February 1987

66 Change

Change is inevitable, except from vending machines.

Anon

Nothing holds a company back – and the individuals
working in it – more than a lack of interest in positive
change. You cannot stand still: you either go
backwards or forwards.

John Adair, academic (1934–)

Tradesmen are not the same as they used to be,
apprentices are not the same, business is not the
same, business commodities are not the same.
Seven-eighths of my stock is old-fashioned. I am an

old-fashioned man in an old-fashioned shop, in a
street that is not the same as I remember it. I have
fallen behind the time, and am too old to catch it
again.

Charles Dickens, novelist (1812–70), *Dombey & Son*
(1846–48)

Change almost never fails because it's too early. It
almost always fails because it's too late.

Seth Godin, entrepreneur (1960–), *Tribes: We Need You to
Lead Us* (2008)

There is at least one point in the history of any
company when you have to change dramatically to
rise to the next level of performance. Miss that
moment and you start to decline.

Andrew Grove, businessman (1936–)

Sitting monarchs don't usually lead revolutions. Yet
most management systems give a disproportionate
share of influence over strategy and policy to a small
number of senior executives. Ironically, these are the
people most vested in the status quo and most likely
to defend it. That's why incumbents often surrender
the future to upstarts. The only solution is to develop
management systems that redistribute power to
those who have most of their emotional equity
invested in the future and have the least to lose from
change.

Gary Hamel, management thinker (1954–), *Harvard Business
Review*, April 2010

So far as the international system is concerned, wealth and power, or economic strength and military strength, are always relative ... and since all societies are subject to the inexorable tendency to change, then the international balances can never be still.

Paul Kennedy, historian (1945–), *The Rise and Fall of the Great Powers* (1987)

Change everything but your wife and children.

Lee Kun-Hee, chairman of Samsung (1942–), speech to managers, 1993

The incremental approach to change is effective when what you want is more of what you've already got.

Richard Pascale, academic (1936–)

Changing the direction of a large company is like trying to turn an aircraft carrier. It takes a mile before anything happens. And if it was a wrong turn, getting back on course takes even longer.

Al Ries, marketing consultant (1926–), *Positioning: The Battle for Your Mind* (2000)

People don't resist change. They resist being changed.

Peter Senge, scientist (1947–), *The Fifth Discipline: The Art and Practice of The Learning Organization* (1990)

Collaboration is vital to sustain what we call profound or really deep change, because without it, organisations are just overwhelmed by the forces of the status quo.

Peter Senge

The only man I know who behaves sensibly is my tailor; he takes my measurements anew each time he sees me. The rest go on with their old measurements and expect me to fit them.

George Bernard Shaw, playwright (1856–1950), *Man and Superman*

Change before you have to.

Jack Welch, businessman (1935–), *Six Rules for Successful Leadership*

66 Civility

Politeness and civility are the best capital ever invested in business.

P.T. Barnum, showman (1810–91), *The Art of Money Getting* (1880)

It is very vulgar to talk about one's business. Only people like stockbrokers do that, and then merely at dinner parties.

Oscar Wilde, writer (1854–1900), *The Importance of Being Earnest*

Joking aside: five quotes from comedians

If I was as rich as Rockefeller I'd be richer than Rockefeller, because I'd do a bit of window cleaning on the side.

Ronnie Barker

Hard work never killed anyone, but why take a chance?

Edgar Bergen

Oh, you hate your job? Why didn't you say so? There's a support group for that. It's called everybody, and they meet at the bar.

Drew Carey

This job is all about application. Of the arse to the chair.

Richard Herring

A good rule of thumb is if you've made it to thirty-five and your job still requires you to wear a name tag, you've made a serious vocational error.

Dennis Miller

❝ Committees

I've searched all the parks in all the cities – and found no statues of committees.

G.K. Chesterton, writer (1874–1936)

If you see a snake, just kill it – don't appoint a committee on snakes.

Ross Perot, businessman and American presidential candidate (1930–)

❝ Communication

It is possible that the telephone has been responsible for more business inefficiency than any other agency except laudanum ... In the old days when you wanted to get in touch with a man you wrote a note, sprinkled it with sand, and gave it to a man on horseback. It probably was delivered within half an hour, depending on how big a lunch the horse had had. But in these busy days of rush-rush-rush, it is sometimes a week before you can catch your man on the telephone.

Robert Benchley, humorist (1889–1945), *One Minute Please!* (1945)

Most emails are biodegradable ... if you let them sink to the bottom of the pile and go unanswered they will eventually become irrelevant.

Guy Browning, humorist (1964–), *Office Politics: How Work Really Works* (2006)

Communication comes in both words and deeds. The latter is generally the most powerful form. Nothing undermines change more than behaviour by important individuals that is inconsistent with the verbal communication.

John Kotter, academic (1947–), *Leading Change* (1996)

The commercial class has always mistrusted verbal brilliancy and wit, deeming such qualities, perhaps with some justice, frivolous and unprofitable.

Dorothy Nevill, writer (1826–1913), *The Reminiscences of Dorothy Nevill* (1906)

The single biggest problem in communication is the illusion that it has taken place.

George Bernard Shaw, playwright (1856–1950)

❝ Communism and socialism

The inherent vice of capitalism is the uneven division of blessings, while the inherent virtue of socialism is the equal division of misery.

Winston Churchill, British prime minister (1874–1965), speech in the House of Commons, 1945

Communism was a great system for making people equally poor – in fact, there was no better system in the world for that than communism. Capitalism made people unequally rich.

Thomas Friedman, writer (1953–), *The World Is Flat 3.0: A Brief History of the Twenty-first Century* (2005)

Political collectivists are no longer much interested in taking things away from the wealthy and creative. Even the most left-wing politicians worship wealth creation – as the political-action-committee collection plate is passed. Partners at Goldman Sachs go forth with their billions. Steve Jobs walks on water. Jay-Z and Beyoncé are rich enough to buy God. Progressive Robin Hoods have turned their attention to robbing ordinary individuals.

P.J. O'Rourke, satirist (1947–), *Wall Street Journal*, April 2011

The world would not be in such a snarl, if Marx had been Groucho instead of Karl.

Irving Thalberg, film producer (1899–1936), birthday message to Groucho Marx

Socialist governments traditionally do make a financial mess. They always run out of other people's money. It's quite a characteristic of them.

Margaret Thatcher, British prime minister (1925–)

66 Competition

The price which society pays for the law of competition ... [is] great; but the advantages of this law are also greater still ... for it is to this law that we owe our wonderful material development, which brings improved conditions in its train. But whether the law be benign or not, we must say of it ... it is here; we cannot evade it; no substitutes for it have been found; and while the law may be sometimes hard for the individual, it is best for the race, because it insures the survival of the fittest in every department.

Andrew Carnegie, businessman (1835–1919), *The Autobiography of Andrew Carnegie and the Gospel of Wealth* (1920)

Goodwill is the one and only asset that competition cannot undersell or destroy.

Marshall Field, businessman (1834–1906)

Out there in some garage is an entrepreneur who's forging a bullet with your company's name on it.

Gary Hamel, management thinker (1954–)

The only way to beat the competition is to stop trying to beat the competition.

W. Chan Kim and **Renée Mauborgne**, *Blue Ocean Strategy* (2005)

In business, the competition will bite you if you keep running, if you stand still, they will swallow you.

William Knusden, businessman (1879–1948)

The trouble with predators is that they don't know who's the prey; until he's dead.

Freddie Laker, airline owner (1922–2006)

Unless you write your competitor's plans, you can't predict the future.

Al Ries and **Jack Trout**, *The 22 Immutable Laws Of Marketing* (1994)

Competition brings out the best in products and the worst in people.

David Sarnoff, businessman (1891–1971)

Every company has a well-defined competitive field of vision, which is usually too narrow. Long periods of equilibrium only exacerbate the problem. A whole raft of "minor little players" operates just at the periphery. They are difficult to see because traditional competitors focus on each other.

Benson Shapiro, **Adrian Slywotzky** and **Richard Tedlow**, "How to Stop Bad Things from Happening to Good Companies", *Strategy+Business*, 1997

Competition is a race, but it's also a race in the mist. Often everyone ends up following the quickest competitor ... but sometimes everybody ends up with a big bump on the head.

Freek Vermeulen, academic, *Business Exposed* (2010)

❝ Complacency

Most men of business think, "Anyhow this system will probably last my time. It has gone on a long time, and is likely to go on still."

Walter Bagehot, businessman, writer and early editor of *The Economist* (1826–77), *Lombard Street: A Description of the Money Market* (1873)

When your company is hugely successful, you don't want to see that the world is changing.

Freek Vermeulen, academic, *Business Exposed* (2010)

❝ Conferences

Conferences are the business equivalent of going for a curry, in that everyone thinks having one is a fantastic idea, but you always end up drinking too much, talking rubbish and feeling sick for days afterwards.

Guy Browning, humorist (1964–), *Office Politics: How Work Really Works* (2006)

No grand idea was ever born in a conference, but a lot of foolish ideas have died there.

F. Scott Fitzgerald, author (1896–1940), letter to France Fitzgerald

❝ Conflict and the arms industry

If you are a gun manufacturer, the product you make is not subject to safety regulation by the Consumer Product Safety Commission. Toy guns are subject to safety regulation; water pistols are, but not real guns.

Michael Barnes, politician (1943–)

Formerly when great fortunes were only made in war, war was business; but now when great fortunes are only made by business: Business is war!

Christian Nestell Bovee, author (1820–1904), *Intuitions and Summaries of Thought* (1862)

I think you will find
When your death takes its toll
All the money you made
Will never buy back your soul.

Bob Dylan, musician (1941–), *Masters of War*

The hidden hand of the market will never work without a hidden fist. McDonald's cannot flourish without McDonnell Douglas, the designer of the F-15. And the hidden fist that keeps the world safe for Silicon Valley's technologies to flourish is called the US Army, Air Force, Navy and Marine Corps.

Thomas Friedman, writer (1953–), *New York Times*, March 1999

Frankly, I'd like to see the government get out of war altogether and leave the whole field to private industry.

Joseph Heller, author (1923–99), *Catch 22* (1961)

The way to make money is to buy when blood is running in the streets.

John D. Rockefeller, industrialist (1839–1937), attributed

66 Consultants and consulting

No one will believe you solved this problem in one day! We've been working on it for months. Now, go act busy for a few weeks and I'll let you know when it's time to tell them.

Anon memo to staff at a software consultancy

A consultant is a man sent in after the battle to bayonet the wounded.

Anon

The acid test of a consultant is whether they can say, "Everything's fine, we'll be off then." No real consultant can. Instead they will sell you a project that costs just enough to keep your profits suppressed to a level that requires further remedial consultancy.

Guy Browning, humorist (1964–), *Office Politics: How Work Really Works* (2006)

A consultant is someone who saves his client almost enough to pay his fee.

Arnold Glasow, humorist (1905–98)

There are designations, like "economist", "prostitute" or "consultant", for which additional characterisation doesn't add information.

Nassim Nicholas Taleb, writer (1960–), *The Bed of Procrustes* (2010)

Consultants are people who borrow your watch and tell you what time it is, and then walk off with your watch.

Robert Townsend, businessman and author (1920–98)

❝ Consumerism

The marriage of reason and nightmare that dominated the 20th century has given birth to an ever more ambiguous world. Across the communications landscape move the spectres of sinister technologies and the dreams that money can buy. Thermo-nuclear weapons systems and soft-drink commercials coexist in an overlit realm ruled by advertising and pseudo-events, science and pornography. Over our lives preside the great twin leitmotifs of the 20th century – sex and paranoia.

J.G. Ballard, author (1930–2009), *Crash* (1973)

We typically misunderstand what's wrong about consumerism. It's not that it makes us love material things too much. To be a good consumer, you have to desire to get lots of things, but you must not love any of them too much once you have them. Consumerism needs children who do not stay attached to their toys for very long and learn to expect the next round of presents as soon as possible.

Phillip Carey, writer, *Good News for Anxious Christians* (2010)

All over the place, from the popular culture to the propaganda system, there is constant pressure to make people feel that they are helpless, that the only role they can have is to ratify decisions and to consume.

Noam Chomsky, linguist (1928–)

The Christmas presents once opened are Not So Much Fun as they were while we were in the process of examining, lifting, shaking, thinking about, and opening them. Three hundred sixty-five days later, we try again and find that the same thing has happened. Each time the goal is reached, it becomes Not So Much Fun, and we're off to reach the next one, then the next one, then the next.

Benjamin Hoff, author (1946–), *The Tao of Pooh* (1982)

We seldom consider how much of our lives we must render in return for some object we barely want, seldom need, buy only because it was put before us.

Ferenc Máté, author (1945–), *A Reasonable Life: Toward a Simpler, Secure, More Humane Existence* (1993)

The consumer isn't a moron; she is your wife.

David Ogilvy, advertising executive (1911–99), *Confessions of an Advertising Man* (1961)

Are these things really better than the things I already have? Or am I just trained to be dissatisfied with what I have now?

Chuck Palahniuk, author (1962–), *Lullaby* (2002)

We're consumers. We are by-products of a lifestyle obsession. Murder, crime, poverty, these things don't concern me. What concerns me are celebrity magazines, television with 500 channels, some guy's name on my underwear.

Chuck Palahniuk, *Fight Club* (1996)

Consumerism: a policy of imposing regulatory burdens on production which hold down the incomes of workers, thereby keeping them from buying things they want that aren't good for them.

Herbert Stein (1916–99), *New York Times Magazine*, 1979

Corporations

Corporation: a miniature totalitarian state governed by a hierarchy of unelected officials who take a dim view of individualism, free speech, equality and eggheads. The backbone of all Western democracies.

Rick Bayan, author (1950–), *The Cynic's Dictionary* (1998)

A corporation does seem like a family ... a hotbed of passion, rivalry, and dreams that build or destroy careers.

Paula Bernstein, author, *Family Ties, Corporate Bonds* (1985)

We were hoping to build a small profitable company; and of course, what we've done is build a large, unprofitable company.

Jeff Bezos, founder of Amazon (1964–), interviewed in 2000

Corporation: an ingenious device for obtaining profit without individual responsibility.

Ambrose Bierce, satirist (1842–1914), *The Devil's Dictionary* (1911)

IBM is like the Stepford Wives. It takes the best people from the best universities and colleges and then snips out some part of the brain so that they become mindless clones.

Bill Campbell, chairman of Intuit, quoted in *Giant Killers* by Geoffrey James (1998)

I believe in God, family, and McDonald's and, in the office, that order is reversed.

Ray Kroc, founder of McDonald's (1902–84), *Grinding It Out* (1977)

Organisations are defined from the inside out: they are described by who reports to whom, by departments and processes and matrices and perks. A business, on the other hand, is defined from the outside in by markets, suppliers, customers, and competitors.

Thomas Stewart, consultant, *Intellectual Capital: The New Wealth of Organizations* (1997)

Organisations are like caffeinated dupes unknowingly jogging backward; you only hear of the few that reach their destination.

Nassim Nicholas Taleb, writer (1960–), *The Bed of Procrustes* (2010)

3 Apples changed the World, 1st one seduced Eve, 2nd fell on Newton and the 3rd was offered to the World half bitten by Steve Jobs.

Twitter user on hearing of Steve Jobs's death, 2011

66 Costs

Watch the costs, and the profits will take care of themselves.

Andrew Carnegie, businessman (1835–1919)

The single most important thing to remember about any enterprise is that results exist only on the outside. The result of a business is a satisfied customer. The result of a hospital is a healed patient. The result of a school is a student who has learned something and puts it to work ten years later. Inside an enterprise, there are only costs.

Peter Drucker, management writer (1909–2005), *The New Realities* (1989)

❝ Creativity

Creativity is allowing yourself to make mistakes. Art is knowing which ones to keep.

Dilbert comic strip

If we listened to our intellect, we'd never have a love affair. We'd never have friendship. We'd never go into business, because we'd be too cynical. Well, that's nonsense. You've got to jump off cliffs all the time and build your wings on the way down.

Annie Dillard, author (1945–)

There can be as much value in the blink of an eye as in months of rational analysis.

Malcolm Gladwell, writer (1963–), *Blink: The Power of Thinking Without Thinking* (2005)

The job is what you do when you are told what to do. The job is showing up at the factory, following instructions, meeting spec, and being managed. Someone can always do your job a little better or faster or cheaper than you can. The job might be difficult, it might require skill, but it's a job. Your art is what you do when no one can tell you exactly how to do it. Your art is the act of taking personal responsibility, challenging the status quo, and changing people. I call the process of doing your art "the work". It's possible to have a job and do the work, too. In fact, that's how you become a linchpin. The job is not the work.

Seth Godin, entrepreneur (1960–), *Linchpin: Are You Indispensable?* (2010)

The difference between a top-flight creative man and the hack is his ability to express powerful meanings indirectly.

Vance Packard, writer (1914–96)

Competition is a by-product of productive work, not its goal. A creative man is motivated by the desire to achieve, not by the desire to beat others.

Ayn Rand, author (1905–82), *Atlas Shrugged* (1957)

The great creators – the thinkers, the artists, the scientists, the inventors – stood alone against the men of their time. Every great new thought was opposed. Every great new invention was denounced. The first motor was considered foolish. The airplane was considered impossible. The power loom was considered vicious. Anaesthesia was considered sinful. But the men of unborrowed vision went ahead. They fought, they suffered and they paid. But they won.

Ayn Rand, *Atlas Shrugged* (1957)

Ideas are like rabbits. You get a couple and learn how to handle them, and pretty soon you have a dozen.

John Steinbeck, author (1902–68), *Conversations with John Steinbeck* edited by Thomas Fensch (1988)

Fast becoming a fixture of organisation life is the meeting self-consciously dedicated to creating ideas. It is a fraud. Much of such high-pressure creation – cooking with gas, creating out loud, spitballing, and so forth – is all very provocative, but if it is stimulating, it is stimulating much like alcohol. After the glow of such a session has worn off, the residue of ideas usually turns out to be a refreshed common denominator everybody is relieved to agree upon – and if there is a new idea, you usually find that it came from a capital of ideas already thought out – by an individual – and perhaps held in escrow until moment for its introduction ... if every member simply wants to do what the group wants to do, then the group is not going to do anything.

William Whyte, writer (1917–99), *The Organization Man* (1956)

Credit

If you have to prove you are worthy of credit, your credit is already gone.

Walter Bagehot, businessman, writer and early editor of *The Economist* (1826–77)

Nothing so cements and holds together all the parts of a society as faith or credit, which can never be kept up unless men are under some force or necessity of honestly paying what they owe to one another.

Marcus Tullius Cicero, philosopher (106–43BC)

Business? It's quite simple: it's other people's money.

Alexandre Dumas, playwright (1824–95), *La Question D'argent*

It is only the poor who pay cash, and that not from virtue, but because they are refused credit.

Anatole France, writer (1844–1924)

I am a most unhappy man. I have unwittingly ruined my country. A great industrial nation is controlled by its system of credit. Our system of credit is concentrated. The growth of the nation, therefore, and all our activities are in the hands of a few men. No longer a government by free opinion, no longer a government by conviction and vote of majority, but a government by the opinion and duress of a small group of dominant men.

Woodrow Wilson, American president (1856–1924), on the Federal Reserve Act, 1913

❝ Crime

[It is] far safer to steal large sums with a pen than small sums with a gun.

Warren Buffett, investor (1930–), *The Essays of Warren Buffett: Lessons for Corporate America* (1998)

I am like any other man. All I do is supply a demand.

Al Capone, gangster (1899–1947)

Why is pot against the law? It wouldn't be because anyone can grow it, and therefore you can't make a profit off it, would it?

Bill Hicks, comedian (1961–94)

A criminal is a person with predatory instincts who has not sufficient capital to form a corporation.

Howard Scott, economist (1926–)

I don't like violence, Tom. I'm a businessman; blood is a big expense.

Sollozzo, character in *The Godfather* (feature film, 1972)

❝ Culture

Company cultures are like country cultures. Never try to change one. Try, instead, to work with what you've got.

Peter Drucker, management writer (1909–2005)

A company's culture is often buried so deeply inside rituals, assumptions, attitudes, and values that it becomes transparent to an organisation's members only when, for some reason, it changes.

Rob Goffee, academic

Customers and customer service

A shoe without sex appeal is like a tree without leaves. Service without emotion is like a shoe without sex appeal.

Anon

You only desire what you cannot get. People want exclusivity, so you must always keep the customer hungry and frustrated.

Jean-Claude Biver, watchmaker (1949–), quoted in *The Economist*

Here is a simple but powerful rule: always give people more than what they expect to get.

Nelson Boswell, author

A consumer is a shopper who is sore about something.

Harold Coffin, writer (1905–81)

The customer is a rear-view mirror, not a guide to the future.

George Colony, founder of Forrester Research (1954–)

Idea Store Canary Wharf

Customer ID: ******9266

Items that you have borrowed

Title: Effective business writing
D: 91000001993799
Due: 02 May 2023

Title: Talk more, say less, get ahead : the
   business speak dictionary
D: 91000008122659
Due: 02 May 2023

Title: The Economist book of business
   quotations
D: 91000001402882
Due: 02 May 2023

Total items: 3
Account balance: £0.00
1/04/2023 13.33
Borrowed: 3
Overdue: 0
Hold requests: 0
Ready for collection: 0

24 hour renewal line: 0333 370 4700
www.ideastore.co.uk

What the customer demands is last year's model, cheaper. To find out what the customer needs you have to understand what the customer is doing as well as he understands it. Then you build what he needs and you educate him to the fact that he needs it.

Nicholas DeWolf, businessman (1928–2006)

There is only one definition of business purpose: to create a customer.

Peter Drucker, management writer (1909–2005), *The Practice of Management* (1954)

You ponce in here, expecting to be waited on hand and foot while I'm trying to run a hotel here! Have you any idea of how much there is to do? Do you ever think of that? Of course not! You're all too busy sticking your noses into every corner, poking around for things to complain about, aren't you? Well, let me tell you something – this is exactly how Nazi Germany started! A lot of layabouts with nothing better to do than to cause trouble! Well, I've had 15 years of pandering to the likes of you, and I've had enough! I've had it! Come on, pack your bags and get out!

Basil Fawlty, character in *Fawlty Towers* (British TV series, 1975–79)

It is not the employer who pays the wages. Employers only handle the money. It is the customer who pays the wages.

Henry Ford, industrialist (1863–1947)

A customer is the most important visitor on our premises. He is not dependent on us. We are dependent on him. He is not an interruption in our work. He is the purpose of it. He is not an outsider in our business. He is part of it. We are not doing him a favour by serving him. He is doing us a favour by giving us an opportunity to do so.

Mahatma Gandhi, Indian nationalist (1868–1948)

Your most unhappy customers are your greatest source of learning.

Bill Gates, founder of Microsoft (1955–), *Business @ the Speed of Thought* (1999)

Letting your customers set your standards is a dangerous game, because the race to the bottom is pretty easy to win. Setting your own standards – and living up to them – is a better way to profit. Not to mention a better way to make your day worth all the effort you put into it.

Seth Godin, entrepreneur (1960–), Seth Godin's blog, July 2006

There's a sucker born every minute.

David Hannum, showman (often misattributed to P.T. Barnum)

When you are skinning your customers you should leave some skin on to grow again so that you can skin them again.

Nikita Khrushchev, Russian president (1894–1971)

Consumers are statistics. Customers are people.

H. Stanley Marcus, businessman (1905–2002)

Customers are not on-off switches, but volume dials.

Don Peppers and **Martha Rogers,** *The One to One Future* (1996)

Without customers, you don't have a business. You have a hobby.

Don Peppers and **Martha Rogers,** *Return on Customer: Creating Maximum Value From Your Scarcest Resource* (2005)

There are no traffic jams along the extra mile.

Roger Staubach, American footballer and businessman (1942–)

Consumer: a person who is capable of choosing a president but incapable of choosing a bicycle without help from a government agency.

Herbert Stein (1916–99), *New York Times Magazine,* 1979

Rule 1: The customer is always right. Rule 2: If the customer is ever wrong, re-read Rule 1.

Motto of Stew Leonard's shops

If you can have it done by Wednesday, say you'll have it done by Friday. Then, deliver it on Tuesday.

Richard Templar, *The Rules of Work: The Unspoken Truth About Getting Ahead in Business*

There is only one boss. The customer. And he can fire everybody in the company from the chairman on down, simply by spending his money somewhere else.

Sam Walton, businessman (1918–92)

66 Cynicism

Scratch the surface of most cynics and you find a frustrated idealist – someone who made the mistake of converting his ideals into expectations.

Peter Senge, scientist (1947–), *The Fifth Discipline: The Art and Practice of The Learning Organization* (1990)

What is a cynic? A man who knows the price of everything and the value of nothing.

Oscar Wilde, writer (1854–1900), *Lady Windermere's Fan*

D

❝ Data, information and statistics

There is a profound difference between information and meaning.
Warren Bennis, academic (1925–)

If you torture the data long enough, it will confess.
Ronald Coase, economist (1910–)

Utility is our national shibboleth: the saviour of the American businessman is fact and his uterine half-brother, statistics.
Edward Dahlberg, novelist (1900–77), *The Carnal Myth* (1968)

In God we trust; all others must bring data.
W. Edwards Deming, statistician (1900–93)

Facts from paper are not the same as facts from people. The reliability of the people giving you the facts is as important as the facts themselves.
Harold Geneen, businessman (1910–97)

Just one cognitive ability distinguished star performers from average: pattern recognition, the "big-picture" thinking that allows leaders to pick out the meaningful trends from the welter of information around them and to think strategically far into the future.

Daniel Goleman, psychologist (1946–), *Emotional Intelligence* (1996)

If you can't measure it, you can't manage it

David Norton and **Robert Kaplan**, *The Balanced Scorecard* (1996)

Most analysts overestimate the importance of scale and underestimate the inertia of buyers.

Richard Rumelt, academic (1942–), *Wall Street Journal*, September 2007

No great marketing decisions have ever been made on qualitative data.

John Sculley, businessman (1939–)

In an information-rich world, the wealth of information means a dearth of something else: a scarcity of whatever it is that information consumes. What information consumes is rather obvious: it consumes the attention of its recipients. Hence a wealth of information creates a poverty of attention, and a need to allocate that attention efficiently among the overabundance of information sources that might consume it.

Herbert Simon, political scientist (1916–2001), *Designing Organizations for an Information-Rich World* (1971)

All correct reasoning is a grand system of tautologies, but only God can make direct use of that fact.

Herbert Simon, "The Natural and Artificial Worlds", *Sciences of the Artificial* (1996)

Facts are meaningless. You could use facts to prove anything that's even remotely true!

Homer Simpson, character in *The Simpsons* (American TV series)

Scientific management means a constant search for the facts, the true actualities, and their intelligent, unprejudiced analysis. Thus, and in no other way, policies and their administration are determined. I keep saying to the General Motors organisation that we are prepared to spend any proper amount of money to get the facts. Only by increased knowledge can we progress, perhaps I had better say survive.

Alfred Sloan, industrialist (1875–1966), *Adventures of a White Collar Man* (1941)

❝ Debt

Debt: an ingenious substitute for the chain and whip of the slavedriver.

Ambrose Bierce, satirist (1842–1914), *The Devil's Dictionary* (1911)

Annual income twenty pounds, annual expenditure nineteen nineteen and six, result happiness. Annual income twenty pounds, annual expenditure twenty pounds nought and six, result misery. The blossom is blighted, the leaf is withered, the god of day goes down upon the dreary scene, and – and in short you are forever floored.

Charles Dickens, novelist (1812–70), *David Copperfield* (1849–50)

A man with a surplus can control circumstances, but a man without a surplus is controlled by them, and often has no opportunity to exercise judgment.

Harvey Firestone, businessman (1868–1938)

66 Decision-making

Not to decide is to decide.

Harvey Cox, theologian (1929–), *On Not Leaving It to the Snake* (1967)

The real discipline comes in saying "no" to the wrong opportunities.

Peter Drucker, management writer (1909–2005)

Five frogs are sitting on a log. Four decide to jump off. How many are left? Answer: five. Why? Because there's a difference between deciding and doing.

Mark Feldman and **Michael Spratt**, *Five Frogs on a Log* (2001)

The key to good decision-making is not knowledge. It is understanding. We are swimming in the former. We are desperately lacking in the latter.

Malcolm Gladwell, writer (1963–), *Blink: The Power of Thinking Without Thinking* (2005)

The man who is denied the opportunity of taking decisions of importance begins to regard as important the decisions he is allowed to take.

Cyril Northcote Parkinson, historian (1909–93), *Parkinson's Law* (1957)

If we are all in agreement on the decision – then I propose we postpone further discussion of this matter until our next meeting to give ourselves time to develop disagreement and perhaps gain some understanding of what the decision is all about.

Alfred Sloan, industrialist (1875–1966)

Compromise is usually bad. It should be a last resort. If two departments or divisions have a problem they can't solve and it comes up to you, listen to both sides and then pick one or the other. This places solid accountability on the winner to make it work. Condition your people to avoid compromise.

Robert Townsend, businessman (1920–98), *Up the Organization* (1970)

When two men in business always agree, one of them is unnecessary.

William Wrigley, businessman (1861–1932)

❝ Delegation

No person will make a great business who wants to do it all himself or get all the credit.

Andrew Carnegie, businessman (1835–1919)

Delegating work works, provided the one delegating works, too.

Robert Half, human resources manager

❝ Design

We think the Mac will sell zillions, but we didn't build the Mac for anybody else. We built it for ourselves. We were the group of people who were going to judge whether it was great or not. We weren't going to go out and do market research. We just wanted to build the best thing we could build. When you're a carpenter making a beautiful chest of drawers, you're not going to use a piece of plywood on the back, even though it faces the wall and nobody will ever see it. You'll know it's there, so you're going to use a beautiful piece of wood on the back. For you to sleep well at night, the aesthetic, the quality, has to be carried all the way through.

Steve Jobs, founder of Apple (1955–2011), quoted in *Playboy*, February 1985

Design is a funny word. Some people think design means how it looks. But of course, if you dig deeper, it's really how it works. The design of the Mac wasn't what it looked like, although that was part of it. Primarily, it was how it worked. To design something really well, you have to get it. You have to really grok what it's all about. It takes a passionate commitment to really thoroughly understand something, chew it up, not just quickly swallow it. Most people don't take the time to do that.

Steve Jobs, quoted in *Wired* magazine, October 1996

Good design can't fix broken business models.

Jeffrey Veen, businessman, *Designing the Friendly Skies*, June 2006

❝ Development

There is some reason to fear that the involvement of non-Western peoples in the conflicts of industrial society, long overdue in itself, will be less to the benefit of the liberated peoples than to that of rationally improved production and communications, and a modestly raised standard of living.

Theodor Adorno, sociologist (1903–69)

In a country like India, the "structural adjustment" end of the corporate globalisation project is ripping through people's lives. "Development" projects, massive privatisation, and labour "reforms" are pushing people off their lands and out of their jobs, resulting in a kind of barbaric dispossession that has few parallels in history. Across the world as the "free market" brazenly protects Western markets and forces developing countries to lift their trade barriers, the poor are getting poorer and the rich richer.

Arundhati Roy, author (1961–), *Not Again*

66 Discipline

Work while you work, play while you play – this is a basic rule of repressive self-discipline.

Theodor Adorno, sociologist (1903–69)

66 Dishonesty

The secret of great fortunes without apparent cause is a crime forgotten, for it was properly done.

Honoré de Balzac, author (1799–1850), *Le Père Goriot* (1835)

I have known a vast quantity of nonsense talked about bad men not looking you in the face. Don't trust that conventional idea. Dishonesty will stare honesty out of countenance any day in the week, if there is anything to be got by it.

Charles Dickens, author (1812–70), *Hunted Down* (1859)

The market is a place set apart where men may deceive each other.

Diogenes Laertius, biographer (c300), *Socrates, his predecessors and followers*

Let me give you a tip on a clue to men's characters: the man who damns money has obtained it dishonourably; the man who respects it has earned it.

Ayn Rand, author (1905–82), *Atlas Shrugged* (1957)

Fella in business got to lie an' cheat, but he calls it somepin else. That's what's important. You go steal that tire an' you're a thief, but he tried to steal your four dollars for a busted tire. They call that sound business.

John Steinbeck, author (1902–68), *The Grapes of Wrath* (1939)

There are three ways to make a living in this business: be first, be smarter, or cheat.

John Tuld, character in *Margin Call* (feature film, 2011)

66 Diversity

Diversity and independence are important because the best collective decisions are the product of disagreement and contest, not consensus or compromise.

James Surowiecki, writer (1976–), *The Wisdom of Crowds* (2004)

Downturns and economic turmoil

Frankly, I don't want to see a rapid upturn. I want it to hold until some of these idiotic competitors go bust.

Joseph Bamford, founder of JCB (1961–2001)

If inflation continues to soar, you're going to have to work like a dog just to live like one.

George Gobel, comedian (1919–91)

Never waste a good crisis.

Lee Myung-Bak, South Korean president, quoted in *The Economist*, November 2009

A depression is for capitalism like a good, cold douche.

Joseph Schumpeter, economist (1883–1950)

The main difference between government bailouts and smoking is that in some rare cases the statement "this is my last cigarette" holds true.

Nassim Nicholas Taleb, writer (1960–), *The Bed of Procrustes* (2010)

The drugs industry

From the point of view of the pharmaceutical industry, the AIDS problem has already been solved. After all, we already have a drug which can be sold at the incredible price of $8,000 an annual dose, and which has the added virtue of not diminishing the market by actually curing anyone.

Barbara Ehrenreich, *The Worst Years of Our Lives* (1991)

Pharma industry is the art of making billions from milligrams.

Gerhard Kocher, political scientist (1939–)

E

Economics

Mathematics brought rigor to Economics.
Unfortunately, it also brought mortis.

Kenneth Boulding, economist (1910–93)

Economists are like computers. They need to have
facts punched into them.

Kenneth Boulding

In all recorded history there has not been one
economist who has had to worry about where the
next meal would come from.

Peter Drucker, management writer (1909–2005)

There are 10^{11} stars in the galaxy. That used to be a
huge number. But it's only 100 billion. It's less than
the national deficit. We used to call them
astronomical numbers. Now we should call them
economical numbers.

Richard Feynman, scientist (1918–88)

The curious task of economics is to demonstrate to men how little they really know about what they imagine they can design.

Friedrich Hayek, economist (1899–1992), *The Fatal Conceit: The Errors of Socialism* edited by W.W. Bartley (1988)

The long run is a misleading guide to current affairs. In the long run we are all dead. Economists set themselves too easy, too useless a task if in tempestuous seasons they can only tell us that when the storm is past the ocean is flat again.

John Maynard Keynes, economist (1883–1946), *A Tract on Monetary Reform* (1923)

If economists could manage to get themselves thought of as humble, competent people on a level with dentists, that would be splendid.

John Maynard Keynes, "The Future", *Essays in Persuasion* (1931)

Practical men, who believe themselves to be quite exempt from any intellectual influences, are usually the slaves of some defunct economist. Madmen in authority, who hear voices in the air, are distilling their frenzy from some academic scribbler of a few years back.

Paul Samuelson, economist (1915–2009), *Inside the Economist's Mind* (2006)

If all the economists were laid end to end, they'd never reach a conclusion.

George Bernard Shaw, playwright (1856–1950)

In brief: five epigrams

I love deadlines. I like the whooshing sound they make as they fly by.
Douglas Adams

I've searched all the parks in all the cities – and found no statues of committees.
G.K. Chesterton

Reporter: What are your two favourite words?
Dorothy Parker: I like "cheque" and "enclosed".

For every complex problem there is a simple solution that is wrong.
George Bernard Shaw

It is only by not paying one's bills that one can hope to live in the memory of the commercial classes.
Oscar Wilde

As every individual, therefore, endeavours as much as he can both to employ his capital in the support of domestic industry, and so to direct that industry that its produce may be of the greatest value; every individual necessarily labours to render the annual revenue of the society as great as he can. He generally, indeed, neither intends to promote the public interest, nor knows how much he is promoting it. By preferring the support of domestic to that of foreign industry, he intends only his own security; and by directing that industry in such a manner as its produce may be of the greatest value, he intends only his own gain, and he is in this, as in many other cases, led by an invisible hand to promote an end which was no part of his intention. Nor is it always the worse for the society that it was no part of it. By pursuing his own interest he frequently promotes that of the society more effectually than when he really intends to promote it. I have never known much good done by those who affected to trade for the public good. It is an affectation, indeed, not very common among merchants, and very few words need be employed in dissuading them from it.

Adam Smith, economist (1723–90), *An Inquiry into the Nature and Causes of the Wealth of Nations* (1776)

Wherever there is great property, there is great inequality.

Adam Smith, *An Inquiry into the Nature and Causes of the Wealth of Nations* (1776)

The first lesson of economics is scarcity: there is never enough of anything to fully satisfy all those who want it. The first lesson of politics is to disregard the first lesson of economics.

Thomas Sowell, economist (1930–), *Is Reality Optional? and Other Essays* (1993)

Give me a one-handed economist. All my economists say, on the one hand ... on the other ...
Harry S. Truman, American president (1884–1972)

66 Education

Universities share one characteristic with compulsive gamblers and exiled royalty: there is never enough money to satisfy their desires.
Derek Bok, former president of Harvard University (1930–)

If you think education is expensive, try ignorance.
Derek Bok

The only part of college not mired in tradition is the price,
Ben Wildavsky, academic, quoted in *The Economist*, July 2011

66 Egotism

It's possible, you can never know, that the universe exists only for me. If so, it's sure going well for me, I must admit.
Bill Gates, founder of Microsoft (1955–), quoted in *Time* magazine, January 1997

The worst disease which can afflict executives in their work is not, as popularly supposed, alcoholism; it's egotism.

Harold Geneen, businessman (1910–97)

66 Emerging markets

When I was growing up, my parents told me, "Finish your dinner. People in China and India are starving." I tell my daughters, "Finish your homework. People in India and China are starving for your job."

Thomas Friedman, writer (1953–), *The World Is Flat: a Brief History of the Twenty-First Century* (2005)

Remember, in China if you are one-in-a-million, there's still 1,300 people just like you.

Microsoft saying

66 Entrepreneurs and entrepreneurialism

We are not a perfect opportunity society in the United States. But if we want to approach that ideal, we must define fairness as meritocracy, embrace a system that rewards merit, and work tirelessly for true equal opportunity. The system that makes this possible, of course, is free enterprise. When I work harder or longer hours in the free-enterprise system, I am generally paid more than if I work less in the same job. Investments in my education translate into

market rewards. Clever ideas usually garner more rewards than bad ones, as judged not by a politburo, but by citizens in the marketplace.
Arthur Brooks, social scientist, *Washington Post*, April 2011

Most entrepreneurs fail because you are working IN your business rather than ON your business.
Michael Gerber, writer, *The E-Myth* (1990)

The entrepreneur in us sees opportunities everywhere we look, but many people see only problems everywhere they look. The entrepreneur in us is more concerned with discriminating between opportunities than he or she is with failing to see the opportunities.
Michael Gerber, *The E-Myth* (1990)

We are so caught in the myths of the best and the brightest and the self-made that we think outliers spring naturally from the earth. We look at the young Bill Gates and marvel that our world allowed that 13-year-old to become a fabulously successful entrepreneur. But that's the wrong lesson. Our world only allowed one 13-year-old unlimited access to a time sharing terminal in 1968. If a million teenagers had been given the same opportunity, how many more Microsofts would we have today? To build a better world we need to replace the patchwork of lucky breaks and arbitrary advantages that today determine success – the fortunate birth dates and the

happy accidents of history – with a society that
provides opportunities for all.

Malcolm Gladwell, writer (1963–), *Outliers: The Story of
Success* (1976)

I told my children when they were leaving education
that they would be well advised to look for
customers not bosses.

Charles Handy, management thinker (1932–), *The Empty
Raincoat* (1994)

A genius is a man who takes the lemons that Fate
hands him and starts a lemonade stand with them.

Elbert Hubbard, philosopher (1856–1915), quoted in *Reader's
Digest*, October 1927

I reckon one entrepreneur can recognise another at
300 yards on a misty day.

Peter Parker, businessman (1924–2002)

If your aspirations are not greater than your
resources, you're not an entrepreneur.

C.K. Prahalad, academic (1941–2010), *Strategy+Business*,
2009

Nobody talks about entrepreneurship as survival, but
that's exactly what it is and what nurtures creative
thinking. Running that first shop taught me business

is not financial science; it's about trading: buying and selling.

Anita Roddick, businesswoman (1949–2007), quoted in *Women at Work* edited by Anna Maslin (2005)

My son is now an "entrepreneur". That's what you're called when you don't have a job.

Ted Turner, media mogul (1938–)

66 The environment

With laissez-faire and price atomic,
Ecology's Uneconomic,
But with another kind of logic
Economy's Unecologic.

Kenneth Boulding, economist (1910–93), *The Careless Technology* (1973)

Modern technology
Owes ecology
An apology.

Alan Eddison, environmentalist, *Worse Verse* (1969)

The only engine big enough to impact Mother Nature is Father Greed.

Thomas Friedman, writer (1953–), *New York Times*, December 2009

The natural capital is not income, but we spend our natural capital as if it were revenue, as if it were going to come back next year without any problems.
Susan George, political scientist (1934–), interview with the Transnational Institute

The best thing we can do with environmentalists is shoot them. These headbangers want to make air travel the preserve of the rich. They are Luddites marching us back to the 18th century.
Michael O'Leary, CEO of Ryanair (1961–)

Envy and jealousy

He who goes unenvied shall not be admired.
Aeschylus, tragedian (c525–c455BC)

Many speak the truth when they say that they despise riches, but they mean the riches possessed by other men.
Charles Caleb Colton, cleric (1780–1832)

Probably the greatest harm done by vast wealth is the harm that we of moderate means do ourselves when we let the vices of envy and hatred enter deep into our natures.
Theodore Roosevelt, American president (1858–1919)

66 Ethics

International business may conduct its operations with scraps of paper, but the ink it uses is human blood.

Eric Ambler, author (1909–98), *A Coffin for Dimitrios* (1939)

You cannot adhere to the teachings of the church on Sunday and not apply them to the marketplace on Monday.

Archbishop LeRoy Bailey junior (1946–)

In the field of modern business, so rich in opportunity for the exercise of man's finest and most varied mental faculties and moral qualities, mere money-making cannot be regarded as the legitimate end. Neither can mere growth of bulk or power be admitted as a worthy ambition. Nor can a man nobly mindful of his serious responsibilities to society view business as a game; since with the conduct of business human happiness or misery is inextricably interwoven.

Louis Brandeis, lawyer (1856–1941), *La Follette's Weekly Magazine*, November 1912

Be Luke Skywalker, not Darth Vader. Ultimately love is stronger than evil.

Donald Burr, founder of People Express (1941–)

In making judgments, the early kings were perfect, because they made moral principles the starting point of all their undertakings and the root of everything was beneficial. This principle, however, is something that people of mediocre intellect never grasp. Not grasping it, they lack awareness, and lacking awareness they pursue profit.

Lü Buwei, merchant (291–235BC), *The annals of Lü Buwei*

Such is the brutalisation of commercial ethics in this country that no one can feel anything more delicate than the velvet touch of a soft buck.

Raymond Chandler, author (1888–1959)

A business that makes nothing but money is a poor business.

Henry Ford, industrialist (1863–1947)

Some day the ethics of business will be universally recognised, and in that day business will be seen to be the oldest and most useful of all the professions.

Henry Ford, *My Life and Work*

There is one and only one responsibility of business – to use its resources and engage in activities designed to increase its profits so long as it stays within the rules of the game.

Milton Friedman, economist (1912–2006), *New York Times*, September 1970

Honour sinks where commerce long prevails.

Oliver Goldsmith, playwright (1730–74), *The Traveller*

Don't be evil.

Google mantra

We actually did an evil scale and decided not to serve at all was worse evil.

Eric Schmidt, former CEO of Google, talking at Davos about offering a censored version of its search engine in China, January 2006

Without commonly shared and widely entrenched moral values and obligations, neither the law, nor democratic government, nor even the market economy will function properly.

Vaclav Havel, playwright and statesman (1936–2011), *Summer Meditations* (1992)

If when a businessman speaks of minority employment, or air pollution, or poverty, he speaks in the language of a certified public accountant analysing a corporate balance sheet, who is to know that he understands the human problems behind the statistical ones? If the businessman would stop talking like a computer printout or a page from the corporate annual report, other people would stop thinking he had a cash register for a heart. It is as simple as that – but that isn't simple.

Louis Lundborg, writer (died 1981), *The Voices of Business* (1979)

There is no such thing as a minor lapse of integrity.

Tom Peters, management writer (1942–), *The Tom Peters Seminar: Crazy Times Call For Crazy Organizations*

Men that have much business must have much pardon.

Proverb

Next to doing the right thing, the most important thing is to let people know you are doing the right thing.

John D. Rockefeller, industrialist (1839–1937)

Ethics and religion must not stay at home when we go to work.

Cardinal Achille Silvestrini (1923–)

66 Europe

The rough broad difference between the American and the European businessman is that the latter is anxious to leave his work, while the former is anxious to get to it.

Arnold Bennett, writer (1867–1931)

Reporter: Mr Kane, how did you find business conditions in Europe?

Charles Foster Kane: How did I find business conditions in Europe? With great difficulty.

Citizen Kane (feature film, 1941)

When an American heiress wants to buy a man, she at once crosses the Atlantic. The only really materialistic people I have ever met have been Europeans.

Mary McCarthy, author (1912–89), *America the Beautiful*

Companies are not charitable enterprises: they hire workers to make profits. In the United States, this logic still works. In Europe, it hardly does.

Paul Samuelson, economist (1915–2009), *Newsweek*, March 1994

66 Experience

If you don't kill a lot of plants along the way, you don't know how to garden

Carol Bartz, businesswoman (1948–)

An optimist is simply a pessimist with no job experience.

Dilbert comic strip

If money is your hope for independence you will never have it. The only real security that a man will have in this world is a reserve of knowledge, experience, and ability.

Henry Ford, industrialist (1863–1947)

In the business world, everyone is paid in two coins:
cash and experience. Take the experience first; the
cash will come later.

Harold Green, businessman (1892–1951)

Good judgment comes from experience, and
experience comes from bad judgment.

Mulla Nasreddin, Middle-Eastern folk hero

We learn best from experience but we never directly
experience the consequences of many of our most
important decisions.

Peter Senge, scientist (1947–), *The Fifth Discipline: The Art
and Practice of The Learning Organization* (1990)

❝ Expertise

An expert is a man who has made all the mistakes
which can be made in a very narrow field.

Niels Bohr, scientist (1885–1962)

It is not enough to do your best; you must know
what to do, and then do your best.

W. Edwards Deming, statistician (1990–93)

Technical people respond to questions in three ways:
It is technically impossible (meaning: I don't feel like
doing it); it depends (meaning: abandon all hope of a
useful answer); the data bits are flexed through a

collectimiser which strips the flow-gate arrays into virtual message elements (meaning: I don't know).

Dilbert comic strip

Talkers are usually more articulate than doers, since talk is their specialty.

Thomas Sowell, economist (1930–), *Ever Wonder Why? and Other Controversial Essays* (2006)

F

66 Failure

Ever tried. Ever failed. No matter. Try Again. Fail again. Fail better.

Samuel Beckett, playwright (1906–89)

It doesn't matter how many times you fail. It doesn't matter how many times you almost get it right. No one is going to know or care about your failures, and neither should you. All you have to do is learn from them and those around you. All that matters in business is that you get it right once. Then everyone can tell you how lucky you are.

Mark Cuban, businessman and basketball team owner (1958–), *How to Win at the Sport of Business: If I Can Do It, You Can Do It* (2011)

Many of life's failures are people who did not realise how close they were to success when they gave up.

Thomas Edison, inventor (1847–1931)

Failure is simply the opportunity to begin again, this time more intelligently.

Henry Ford, industrialist (1863–1947)

If you try to do something and fail, you are vastly better off than if you had tried nothing and succeeded.

Fortune cookie motto

The secret to being wrong isn't to avoid being wrong! The secret is being willing to be wrong. The secret is realising that wrong isn't fatal.

Seth Godin, entrepreneur (1960–), *Linchpin: Are You Indispensable?* (2010)

A failure is a man who has blundered, but is not able to cash in the experience.

Elbert Hubbard, philosopher (1856–1915), *The Philistine*

If you don't fail at least 90% of the time, you're not aiming high enough.

Alan Kay, computer scientist (1940–)

We have forty million reasons for failure, but not a single excuse.

Rudyard Kipling, author (1865–1936), "The Lesson", the *Times*, July 1901

The common idea that success spoils people by making them vain, egotistic, and self-complacent is erroneous; on the contrary it makes them, for the most part, humble, tolerant, and kind. Failure makes people bitter and cruel.

W. Somerset Maugham, novelist (1874–1965)

Showing character: five quotes from film and TV

All I've ever wanted was an honest week's pay for an honest day's work.

Sergeant Ernest Bilko, character in *Sergeant Bilko*

Reporter: Mr Kane, how did you find business conditions in Europe?

Charles Foster Kane: How did I find business conditions in Europe? With great difficulty.

Citizen Kane

If you don't like what's being said, change the conversation.

Donald Draper, character in *Mad Men*

The point is ladies and gentlemen that greed, for lack of a better word, is good.

Gordon Gekko, character in *Wall Street*

I don't like violence, Tom. I'm a businessman; blood is a big expense.

Sollozzo, character in *The Godfather*

Fail! Fast. Then succeed
Wired magazine cover, 2011

❝ Family business

Nobody talks more of free enterprise and
competition and of the best man winning than the
man who inherited his father's store or farm.
C. Wright Mills, sociologist (1917–61), *White Collar: The
American Middle Class* (1951)

In a family business, it's the third generation that
presents the big problems. The first generation
founds the company and has the drive and the
dedication to move it forward. The second
generation rides that wave. The third generation
wants to do their own thing. They've seen Broadway;
they've had all the advantages.
Gale Petronis, businesswoman

❝ The film industry

No wonder the film industry started in the desert in
California where, like all desert dwellers, they dream
their buildings, rather than design them.
Arthur Erickson, architect (1924–2009)

In this industry, there are only two ways up the ladder. Rung by rung or claw your way to the top. It's sure been tough on my nails.

Jack Nicholson, actor (1937–)

Hollywood is the only industry, even taking in soup companies, which does not have laboratories for the purpose of experimentation.

Orson Welles, actor and film director (1915–85)

66 Financial crises

There are no atheists in foxholes and no ideologues in financial crises.

Ben Bernanke, economist (1953–), chairman of the US Federal Reserve (2008)

When I hear "Chinese wall", I think, "You're a fucking liar".

Vincent Daniel, hedge fund manager, quoted in *The Big Short* by Michael Lewis (2010)

When a fight breaks out in a bar, you don't hit the man who started it. You clobber the person you don't like instead.

Fund manager, quoted in *The Economist*, November 2009

Is it possible to be both terrified and bored?

Paul Krugman, economist (1953–), commenting on the financial crisis, *Huffington Post*, September 2011

Everything, in retrospect, is obvious. But if everything were obvious, authors of histories of financial folly would be rich.

Michael Lewis, author (1960–), *Panic!: The Story of Modern Financial Insanity* (2008)

❝ Following the herd

Most managers have very little incentive to make the intelligent-but-with-some-chance-of-looking-like-an-idiot decision. Their personal gain/loss ratio is all too obvious: if an unconventional decision works out well, they get a pat on the back and, if it works out poorly, they get a pink slip. (Failing conventionally is the route to go; as a group, lemmings may have a rotten image, but no individual lemming has ever received bad press.)

Warren Buffett, investor (1930–), letter to the shareholders of Berkshire Hathaway

Ever wonder why fund managers can't beat the S&P 500? 'Cause they're sheep, and sheep get slaughtered.

Gordon Gekko, character in *Wall Street* (feature film, 1987)

66 Foot-in-mouth and blunt honesty

I would buy a Mac if I didn't work for Microsoft.

Jim Allchin, Microsoft development executive (1951–), e-mail (2004)

I do not borrow [on Barclaycard] because it is too expensive ... I have four young children. I give them advice not to pile up debts on their credit cards.

Matthew Barratt, CEO of Barclaycard (1944–)

[We] sold a pair of earrings for under a pound, which is cheaper than a prawn sandwich from Marks & Spencer, but probably wouldn't last as long ... We also do cut-glass sherry decanters complete with six glasses on a silver-plated tray that your butler can serve you drinks on, all for £4.95. People say, "How can you sell this for such a low price?" I say, because it's total crap.

Gerald Ratner, jeweller (1949–)

Why in the world would you think your [mobile] phone would work in your house? The customer has come to expect so much.

Ivan Seidenberg, former CEO of Verizon (1946–), quoted in the *San Francisco Chronicle*, April 2005

[Our target customers] are football hooligans ... very few of our customers have to wear suits to work. They'll be for his first interview or first court appearance

David Shepherd, brand director of Topman

Newcastle girls are all dogs.

Freddie Shepherd, chairman of Newcastle Football Club (1942–)

66 Friendship

Family, religion, friends ... these are the three demons you must slay if you wish to succeed in business.

Monty Burns, character in *The Simpsons* (American TV series)

Friends and money: oil and water.

Michael Corleone, character in *The Godfather* (feature film, 1972)

If you want a friend, get a dog.

Gordon Gekko, character in *Wall Street* (feature film, 1987) – originally attributed to Harry Truman

All lasting business is built on friendship.

Alfred Montapert, author

A friendship founded on business is a good deal better than a business founded on friendship.

John D. Rockefeller, industrialist (1839–1937)

 Fulfilment

Unless a man believes in himself and makes a total commitment to his career and puts everything he has into it – his mind, his body, his heart – what's life worth to him?

Vince Lombardi, American football coach (1913–70)

A good rule of thumb is if you've made it to 35 and your job still requires you to wear a name tag, you've made a serious vocational error.

Dennis Miller, comedian (1953–)

Fun

Business is more exciting than any game.

Lord Beaverbrook, tycoon (1879–1964)

Creative ideas flourish best in a shop which preserves some spirit of fun. Nobody is in business for fun, but that does not mean there cannot be fun in business.

Leo Burnett, advertising executive (1891–1971)

I want to put a ding in the universe.

Steve Jobs, founder of Apple (1955–2011)

Men always try to keep women out of business so they won't find out how much fun it really is.

Vivien Kellems, industrialist (1896–1975), quoted in *Women can be Engineers* by Alice Goff (1946)

G

❝ Gambling

The gambling known as business looks with austere disfavour upon the business known as gambling.

Ambrose Bierce, satirist (1842–1914), *The Devil's Dictionary* (1911)

The sort of project God would build if he had the money.

A competitor's description of MGM Mirage's CityCenter in Las Vegas Strip, quoted in *The Economist*, 2009

In the casino, the cardinal rule is to keep them playing and to keep them coming back. The longer they play, the more they lose, and in the end, we get it all.

Sam "Ace" Rothstein, character in *Casino* (feature film, 1995)

❝ Globalisation

Internationalisation is like creating a round-toed shoe that fits people with all types of feet. It is not as comfortable as a perfectly fitted shoe and doesn't fit snugly, but can be worn by many people.

David DeBry, "Globalizing Instructional Materials: Guidelines for Higher Education", *TechTrends*, December 2007

Despite different cultures, middle-class youth all over the world seem to live their lives as if in a parallel universe. They get up in the morning, put on their Levi's and Nikes, grab their caps and backpacks, and Sony personal CD players and head for school.

Naomi Klein, author (1970–), *No Logo: Taking Aim at the Brand Bullies* (1999)

The Earth is round but, for most purposes, it's sensible to treat it as flat.

Theodore Levitt, academic (1925–2006), "The Globalisation of Markets", *Harvard Business Review*, May 1983

The extension and use of railroads, steamships, telegraphs, break down nationalities and bring peoples geographically remote into close connection commercially and politically. They make the world one, and capital, like water, tends to a common level.

David Livingstone, missionary (1813–73), *The Last Journals of David Livingstone*

Think globally, act locally.

Akio Morita, co-founder of Sony (1921–99)

The word "overseas" has no place in Honda's vocabulary, because it sees itself as equidistant from all its key customers.

Kenichi Ohmae, management thinker (1943–), *The Borderless World* (1990)

People have accused me of being in favour of globalisation. This is equivalent to accusing me of being in favour of the sun rising in the morning.

Clare Short, politician (1946–)

Greed

Avarice begins where poverty ends.

Honoré de Balzac, author (1799–1850), *La Comédie Humaine* (1779–1850)

I will tell you the secret to getting rich on Wall Street. Close the doors. You try to be greedy when others are fearful. And you try to be fearful when others are greedy.

Warren Buffett, investor (1930–), quoted in *Buffett: The Making of an American Capitalist* by Roger Lowenstein (1995)

If it weren't for greed, intolerance, hate, passion and murder, you would have no works of art, no great buildings, no medical science, no Mozart, no Van Gogh, no Muppets and no Louis Armstrong.

Jasper Fforde, author (1961–), *The Big Over Easy* (2005)

Earth provides enough to satisfy every man's need, but not every man's greed.
Mahatma Gandhi, Indian nationalist (1869–1948)

The point is ladies and gentlemen that greed, for lack of a better word, is good.
Gordon Gekko, character in *Wall Street* (feature film, 1987)

Although gold dust is precious, when it gets in your eyes it obscures your vision
Hsi Tang Chih Tsang, monk (735–814)

It's true: greed has had a very bad press. I frankly don't see anything wrong with greed. I think that the people who are always attacking greed would be more consistent with their position if they refused their next salary increase ... greed simply means that you are trying to relieve the nature given scarcity that man was born with. Greed will continue until the Garden of Eden arrives, when everything is superabundant, and we don't have to worry about economics at all.
Murray Rothbard, economist (1926–95), *Economic Controversies* (2011)

66 Growth

Dishonest money dwindles away, but he who gathers money little by little makes it grow.
The Bible, Proverbs 13:11

Anyone who believes exponential growth can go on forever in a finite world is either a madman or an economist.

Kenneth Boulding, economist (1910–93)

Without continual growth and progress, such words as improvement, achievement, and success have no meaning.

Benjamin Franklin, polymath (1705–90)

Great things do not just happen by impulse but are a succession of small things linked together.

Vincent van Gogh, artist (1853–90), Letter to Theo van Gogh, October 1882

Think and act big and grow smaller, or think and act small and grow bigger.

Herb Kelleher, founder of Southwest Airlines (1931–), quoted in *USA Today*, June 1994

The meek shall inherit the earth, but they'll never increase market share.

William McGovan, entrepreneur (1927–92)

The American Beauty Rose can be produced in the splendour and fragrance which brings cheer to its beholder only by sacrificing the early buds which grow up around it. This is not an evil tendency in business. It is merely the working-out of a law of nature and a law of God.

John D. Rockefeller junior, industrialist (1874–1960), quoted in *The History of the Standard Oil Company* by Ida Tarbell (1904)

H

 Happiness

Happiness is not just a mood – it's a work ethic
Shawn Achor, teacher and writer, *The Happiness Advantage: The Seven Principles of Positive Psychology That Fuel Success and Performance at Work* (2010)

Happiness is obsolete: uneconomic.
Theodor Adorno, sociologist (1903–69)

One day's happiness often predicts the next day's creativity.
Teresa Amabile, psychologist (1950–)

Choose a job you love and you will never have to work a day in your life.
Confucius, philosopher (551–479BC)

One should guard against preaching to young people success in the customary form as the main aim of life. The most important motive for work in school and in life is pleasure in work, pleasure in its result, and the knowledge of the result to the community.
Albert Einstein, scientist (1879–1955)

Transferring your passion to your job is far easier than finding a job that happens to match your passion.

Seth Godin, entrepreneur (1960–), *Linchpin: Are You Indispensable?* (2010)

We have no more right to consume happiness without producing it than to consume wealth without producing it.

George Bernard Shaw, playwright (1856–1950), *Candida*

Hard work

Fortune cannot be flattered by such fetish worship. But she can be wooed and won by hard work.

Lord Beaverbrook, tycoon (1879–1964)

Hard work never killed anybody, but why take a chance?

Edgar Bergen, ventriloquist (1903–78)

Go to the ant, thou sluggard; consider her ways, and be wise: which having no guide, overseer, or ruler, provideth her meat in the summer, and gathereth her food in the harvest.

The Bible, Proverbs 6:6–8

Seest thou a man diligent in his business? He shall stand before kings; he shall not stand before mean men.

The Bible, Proverbs 22:29.

In art and enterprise, it is the steady, silent work that does the work.

Christian Nestell Bovee (1820–1904), *Intuitions and Summaries of Thought* (1862)

The man of business knows that only by years of patient, unremitting attention to affairs can he earn his reward, which is the result, not of chance, but of well-devised means for the attainment of ends.

Andrew Carnegie, businessman (1835–1919), *The Empire of Business* (1902)

The average person puts about 25% of his energy and ability into his work. The world takes off its hat to those who put in more than 50% of their capacity, and stands on its head for those few and far between souls who devote 100%.

Andrew Carnegie

None of my inventions came by accident. I see a worthwhile need to be met and I make trial after trial until it comes. What it boils down to is 1% inspiration and 99% perspiration.

Thomas Edison, inventor (1847–1931)

Opportunity is missed by most people because it is dressed in overalls and looks like work.

Thomas Edison

Hard work is a prison sentence only if it does not have meaning. Once it does, it becomes the kind of thing that makes you grab your wife around the waist and dance a jig.

Malcolm Gladwell, writer (1963–), *Blink: The Power of Thinking Without Thinking* (2005)

No one who can rise before dawn three hundred sixty days a year fails to make his family rich.

Malcolm Gladwell, *Outliers: The Story of Success* (1976)

If you want work well done, select a busy man, the other kind has no time.

Elbert Hubbard, philosopher (1856–1915), *The Philosophy of Elbert Hubbard* (1916)

Industry is a better horse to ride than genius.

Walter Lippman, writer (1889–1974)

Leaders are not born. They are made. They are made just like anything else ... through hard work.

Vince Lombardi, American football coach (1913–70)

Lost wealth may be replaced by industry, lost knowledge by study, lost health by temperance or medicine, but lost time is gone forever.

Samuel Smiles, author (1812–1904), *Self Help* (1859)

People who have time on their hands will inevitably waste the time of people who have work to do.

Thomas Sowell, economist (1930–), *Is Reality Optional? and Other Essays* (1993)

Pennies don't fall from heaven, they have to be earned here on earth.

Margaret Thatcher, British prime minister (1925–)

❝ Hiring

Never hire someone who knows less than you do about what he's hired to do.

Malcolm Forbes, businessman (1919–90)

If you have lower than a 10% turnover, there is a problem. And if you have higher than, say 20%, there is a problem.

William McGovern, writer

When someone is made the head of an office in the Ogilvy & Mather chain, I send him a Matrioshka doll from Gorky. If he has the curiosity to open it, and keep opening it until he comes to the inside of the smallest doll, he finds this message: If each of us hires people who are smaller than we are, we shall become a company of dwarfs. But if each of us hires people who are bigger than we are, we shall become a company of giants.

David Ogilvy, advertising executive (1911–99), *Ogilvy on Advertising* (1983)

Hire character. Train skill.

Peter Schultz, inventor (1942–)

66 Honesty

Is Chapter 11 what comes after following the ten commandments?

Anon

Corruptio optimi pessima. (Corruption of the best is the worst.)

Attributed to **Aristotle**, philosopher (384–322BC)

Commerce is a heaven, whose sun is trustworthiness and whose moon is truthfulness.

Bahá'u'lláh, prophet (1817–92)

For the merchant, even honesty is a financial speculation.

Charles Baudelaire, poet (1821–67), *My Heart Laid Bare* (1865)

Sunlight is the best disinfectant.

Louis Brandeis, lawyer (1856–1941)

The more truth you can get into any business, the better. Let the other side know the defects of yours, let them know how you are to be satisfied, let there be as little to be found as possible (I should say nothing), and if your business be an honest one, it will be best tended in this way.

Arthur Helps, writer (1813–75), *Friends in Council* (1847)

There are certain things that tax your credibility – like the fourth anniversary of a going-out-of-business sale.

Robert Orben, comedy writer (1927–)

Train any population rationally, and they will be rational. Furnish honest and useful employments to those so trained, and such employments they will greatly prefer to dishonest or injurious occupations. It is beyond all calculation the interest of every government to provide that training and that employment, and to provide both is easily practicable.

Robert Owen, social reformer (1771–1858), *A New View of Society* (1816)

An honest man is one who knows that he can't consume more than he has produced.

Ayn Rand, author (1905–82), *Atlas Shrugged* (1957)

In business affairs, it is the manner in which even small matters are transacted that often decides man for or against you.

Samuel Smiles, author (1812–1904), "Men of Business", *Self Help* (1859)

Hubris

In a bull market, one must avoid the error of the preening duck that quacks boastfully after a torrential rainstorm, thinking that its paddling skills have caused it to rise in the world. A right-thinking duck would instead compare its position after the downpour to that of the other ducks on the pond.

Warren Buffett, investor (1930–), letter to the shareholders of Berkshire Hathaway

The next generation begins when we say it does.

Ken Kutagari, chairman of Sony's video-game division (1950–)

I

66 Innovation

Many great ideas have been lost because the people who had them could not stand being laughed at.

Anon

Don't worry about people stealing an idea. If it's original, you will have to ram it down their throats.

Howard Aiken, computer scientist (1899–73), quoted in *Portraits in Silicon* by Robert Slater (1989)

If you think of [opportunity] in terms of the Gold Rush, then you'd be pretty depressed right now because the last nugget of gold would be gone. But the good thing is, with innovation, there isn't a last nugget. Every new thing creates two new questions and two new opportunities.

Jeff Bezos, founder of Amazon (1964–)

Do you realise if it weren't for Edison we'd be watching TV by candlelight?

Al Boliska, radio presenter (1942–72)

It's important not to overstate the benefits of ideas. Quite frankly, I know it's kind of a romantic notion that you're just going to have this one brilliant idea and then everything is going to be great. But the fact is that coming up with an idea is the least important part of creating something great. It has to be the right idea and have good taste, but the execution and delivery are what's key.

Sergey Brin, founder of Google (1973–)

Poor old Spotty Muldoon. He thought of splitting the atom the other day. If only he could have had the idea about 30 years ago, he'd have made a bloody fortune.

Peter Cook, satirist (1937–95), E.L. Wisty, character in *The Man Who Invented the Wheel* (1964)

A surprising number of innovations fail not because of some fatal technological flaw or because the market isn't ready. They fail because responsibility to build these businesses is given to managers or organisations whose capabilities aren't up to the task ... Most often the very skills that propel an organisation to succeed in sustaining circumstances systematically bungle the best ideas for disruptive growth. An organisation's capabilities become its disabilities when disruptive innovation is afoot.

Clayton Christensen, academic (1952–), *The Innovator's Dilemma* (1997)

Large corporations welcome innovation and individualism in the same way the dinosaurs welcomed large meteors.

Dilbert comic strip

Innovation is the specific instrument of entrepreneurship. The act that endows resources with a new capacity to create wealth.

Peter Drucker, management writer (1909–2005), *Innovation and Entrepreneurship* (1985)

All economic activity is by definition "high risk". And defending yesterday – that is, not innovating – is far more risky than making tomorrow.

Peter Drucker, *Innovation and Entrepreneurship* (1985)

Wall Street's graveyards are filled with men who were right too soon.

William Peter Hamilton, newspaper editor (1867–1929)

Many people still believe a better mousetrap is all it takes. But of the 2000+ mousetraps patented, only two have sold well, and they were both designed in the 19th century. A good idea doesn't sell itself although most "lone inventors" make the mistake of thinking it will.

Andrew Hargadon, academic, *How Breakthroughs Happen: The Surprising Truth About How Companies Innovate* (2003)

We are more ready to try the untried when what we do is inconsequential. Hence the fact that many inventions had their birth as toys.

Eric Hoffer, philosopher (1902–83)

If it's a good idea, go ahead and do it. It is much easier to apologise than it is to get permission.

Grace Hopper, computer scientist (1906–92)

The world is moving so fast these days that the man who says it can't be done is generally interrupted by someone doing it.

Elbert Hubbard, philosopher (1856–1915)

Innovation comes from people meeting up in the hallways or calling each other at 10.30 at night with a new idea, or because they realised something that shoots holes in how we've been thinking about a problem. It's ad hoc meetings of six people called by someone who thinks he has figured out the coolest new thing ever and who wants to know what other people think of his idea. And it comes from saying no to 1,000 things to make sure we don't get on the wrong track or try to do too much. We're always thinking about new markets we could enter, but it's only by saying no that you can concentrate on the things that are really important.

Steve Jobs, founder of Apple (1955–2011), quoted in *BusinessWeek*, May 1998

The best way to predict the future is to invent it.

Alan Kay, computer scientist (1940–)

Only puny secrets need protection. Big discoveries are protected by public incredulity.

Marshall McLuhan, teacher and philosopher (1911–80), *Take Today: The Executive as Dropout* (1972)

Invention is the mother of necessities.

Marshall McLuhan, "The Argument: Causality in the Electric World", *Technology and Culture: Symposium* 14 (1), January 1973

In big industry new ideas are invited to rear their heads so they can be clobbered at once. The idea department of a big firm is a sort of lab for isolating dangerous viruses.

Marshall McLuhan

The protections for the imagination are indiscriminate. They shield bad ideas as well as good ones – and there are many more of the former than the latter. Most fantasies lead us astray, and most of the consequences of imagination for individuals and individual organisations are disastrous.

James March, academic (1928–)

The public does not know what is possible. We do.

Akio Morita, co-founder of Sony (1921–99)

If it ain't broke, break it.

Richard Pascale, academic (1938–), *Managing on the Edge* (1990)

Ideas rose in clouds; I felt them collide until pairs interlocked, so to speak, making a stable combination.

Henri Poincaré, mathematician (1854–1912), *Essay on the Psychology of Invention in the Mathematical Field*

Invention consists in avoiding the constructing of useless contraptions and in constructing the useful combinations which are in infinite minority. To invent is to discern, to choose.

Henri Poincaré

If you can, be first. If you can't be first, create a new category in which you can be first.

Al Ries and **Jack Trout**, *The 22 Immutable Laws Of Marketing* (1994)

Reactive innovation does little to differentiate a company from the competition, and just delays the sinking of the ship. Innovation must be pervasive and perpetual: everyone, everywhere, all of the time. Innovation must be seen as the key currency within the company.

Stephen Shapiro, consultant, *24/7 Innovation* (2002)

Insurance

Americans have an abiding belief in their ability to control reality by purely material means ... airline insurance replaces the fear of death with the comforting prospect of cash.

Cecil Beaton, photographer (1904–80)

In the insurance business, there is no statute of limitation on stupidity.

Warren Buffett, investor (1930–)

For almost 70 years the life insurance industry has been a smug sacred cow feeding the public a steady line of sacred bull.

Ralph Nader, activist (1934–), quoted in the *New York Times*, May 1974

The internet

If you make customers unhappy in the physical world, they might each tell six friends. If you make customers unhappy on the internet, they can each tell 6,000 friends.

Jeff Bezos, founder of Amazon (1964–)

They say a year in the internet business is like a dog year, equivalent to seven years in a regular person's life.

Vinton Cerf, father of the internet (1943–)

Let's face it. We're not changing the world. We're building a product that helps people buy more crap – and watch porn.

Bill Watkins, former CEO of Seagate Technologies (1953–), *Fortune*, November 2006

❝ Intuition

You can't connect the dots looking forward; you can only connect them looking backwards. So you have to trust that the dots will somehow connect in your future. You have to trust in something – your gut, destiny, life, karma, whatever. This approach has never let me down, and it has made all the difference in my life.

Steve Jobs, founder of Apple (1955–2011), Stanford commencement speech (2005)

Leaders trust their guts. "Intuition" is one of those good words that has gotten a bad rap. For some reason, intuition has become a "soft" notion. Garbage! Intuition is the new physics. It's an Einsteinian, seven-sense, practical way to make tough decisions.

Tom Peters, management writer (1942–), *Fast Company*, February 2001

66 Investing

To turn $100 into $110 is work. To turn $100m into
$110m is inevitable.

Edward Bronfman senior, businessman (1927–2005)

The line separating investment and speculation,
which is never bright and clear, becomes blurred still
further when most market participants have recently
enjoyed triumphs. Nothing sedates rationality like
large doses of effortless money. After a heady
experience of that kind, normally sensible people
drift into behaviour akin to that of Cinderella at the
ball. They know that overstaying the festivities – that
is, continuing to speculate in companies that have
gigantic valuations relative to the cash they are likely
to generate in the future – will eventually bring on
pumpkins and mice. But they nevertheless hate to
miss a single minute of what is one helluva party.
Therefore, the giddy participants all plan to leave just
seconds before midnight. There's a problem, though:
they are dancing in a room in which the clocks have
no hands.

Warren Buffett, investor (1930–), letter to the shareholders
of Berkshire Hathaway

A pin lies in wait for every bubble. And when the
two eventually meet, a new wave of investors learns
some very old lessons. First, many in Wall Street – a
community in which quality control is not prized

– will sell investors anything they will buy. Second, speculation is most dangerous when it looks easiest.

Warren Buffett, letter to the shareholders of Berkshire Hathaway

You only find out who is swimming naked when the tide goes out.

Warren Buffett, letter to the shareholders of Berkshire Hathaway

One of the ironies of the stock market is the emphasis on activity. Brokers, using terms such as "marketability" and "liquidity", sing the praises of companies with high share turnover (those who cannot fill your pocket will confidently fill your ear). But investors should understand that what is good for the croupier is not good for the customer. A hyperactive stock market is the pickpocket of enterprise.

Warren Buffett, *The Essays of Warren Buffett: Lessons for Investors and Managers* (1998)

Professional investment may be likened to those newspaper competitions in which the competitors have to pick out the six prettiest faces from a hundred photographs, the prize being awarded to the competitor whose choice most nearly corresponds to the average preferences of the competitors as a whole.

John Maynard Keynes, economist (1883–1946), *The General Theory of Employment Interest and Money* (1936)

Those who know don't tell and those who tell don't know.

Michael Lewis, author (1960–), *The Big Short* (2010)

An important key to investing is to remember that stocks are not lottery tickets.

Peter Lynch, investor (1944–), *Beating the Street* (1993)

This is not like pure science where you go, "Aha" and you've got the answer. By the time you've got "Aha", Chrysler's already quadrupled or Boeing's quadrupled. You have to take a little bit of risk.

Peter Lynch

Everyone has the brain power to make money in stocks. Not everyone has the stomach.

Peter Lynch

I can calculate the movement of the stars, but not the madness of men.

Isaac Newton, scientist (1642–1727), attributed comment on losing his investment in the South Sea Bubble

Money is the seed of money, and the first guinea is sometimes more difficult to acquire than the second million.

Jean-Jacques Rousseau, philosopher (1712–78), *A Discourse on Political Economy* (1775)

Investing should be more like watching paint dry or watching grass grow. If you want excitement, take $800 and go to Las Vegas.

Paul Samuelson, economist (1915–2009)

October. This is one of the peculiarly dangerous months to speculate in stocks. The others are July, January, September, April, November, May, March, June, December, August and February.

Mark Twain, author (1835–1910), *Pudd'nhead Wilson* (1894)

Like migrating gnus the investors follow each other and the analysts. Sometimes they encounter a ravine on their journey.

Jeroen van der Veer, businessman (1947–)

K

66 Knowledge

[Wisdom is] finally being able to figure out what you should be worrying about and what you shouldn't.

Edward Albee, playwright (1928–)

Insight is not a light bulb that goes off inside our heads. It is a flickering candle that can easily be snuffed out.

Malcolm Gladwell, writer (1963–), *Blink: The Power of Thinking Without Thinking* (2005)

The most sensible people to be met with in society are men of business and of the world, who argue from what they see and know, instead of spinning cobweb distinctions of what things ought to be.

William Hazlitt, writer (1778–1830), *On the Ignorance of the Learned*

A specialist is a man who knows more and more about less and less.

William James Mayo (1861–1939), quoted in *Reader's Digest*, November 1927

If you want to be a leader, you've got to be a reader.

David Noebel, religious leader and writer (1937–)

The best minds are not in government. If any were, business would hire them away.

Ronald Reagan, American president (1911–2004)

Don't be afraid to take time to learn. It's good to work for other people. I worked for others for 20 years. They paid me to learn.

Vera Wang, fashion designer (1949–)

66 Knowledge workers

The great challenge to management today is to make productive the tremendous new resource, the knowledge worker. This, rather than the productivity of the manual worker, is the key to economic growth and economic performance in today's society.

Peter Drucker, management writer (1909–2005), *Concept of the Corporation* (1946)

I'm struck by the insidious, computer-driven tendency to take things out of the domain of muscular activity and put them into the domain of mental activity. The transfer is not paying off. Sure, muscles are unreliable, but they represent several million years of accumulated finesse.

Brian Eno, musician, *Wired* magazine, January 1999

Too often the business world can identify a successful approach only when it sees it. The random odds of success or failure are as significant as their strategies. It's not unusual for a company to hire bright 29-year-old McKinsey consultants and ignore the knowledge and expertise of its own 29-year-old employees.

Gary Hamel, management thinker (1954–), *Workforce Management* blog

L

❝ Labour

Between labour and play stands work. A man is a worker if he is personally interested in the job which society pays him to do; what from the point of view of society is necessary labour is from his point of view voluntary play. Whether a job is to be classified as labour or work depends, not on the job itself, but on the tastes of the individual who undertakes it. The difference does not, for example, coincide with the difference between a manual and a mental job; a gardener or a cobbler may be a worker, a bank clerk a labourer.

W.H. Auden, poet (1907–73), "Work, Labour and Play", *A Certain World: A Commonplace Book* (1970)

A man's labour is not only his capital but his life. When it passes it returns never more. To utilise it, to prevent its wasteful squandering, to enable the poor man to bank it up for use hereafter, this surely is one of the most urgent tasks before civilisation.

William Booth, founder of the Salvation Army (1829–1912), *In Darkest England, and the Way Out* (1890)

Even in the meanest sorts of Labour, the whole soul of a man is composed into a kind of real harmony the instant he sets himself to work.

Thomas Carlyle, historian (1795–1881), *Past and Present* (1843)

You cannot spend money in luxury without doing good to the poor. Nay, you do more good to them by spending it in luxury, than by giving it; for by spending it in luxury, you make them exert industry, whereas by giving it, you keep them idle.

Samuel Johnson, author (1709–84), *The Life of Samuel Johnson* by James Boswell (1791)

Labour alone, therefore, never varying in its own value, is alone the ultimate and real standard by which the value of all commodities can at all times and places be estimated and compared. It is their real price; money is their nominal price only.

Adam Smith, economist (1723–90), *An Inquiry into the Nature and Causes of the Wealth of Nations* (1776)

This division of labour, from which so many advantages are derived, is not originally the effect of any human wisdom, which foresees and intends that general opulence to which it gives occasion. It is the necessary, though very slow and gradual, consequence of a certain propensity in human nature, which has in view no such extensive utility;

the propensity to truck, barter, and exchange one
thing for another.

Adam Smith, *An Inquiry into the Nature and Causes of the
Wealth of Nations* (1776)

In the long run the workman may be as necessary to
his master as his master is to him, but the necessity is
not so immediate.

Adam Smith, *An Inquiry into the Nature and Causes of the
Wealth of Nations* (1776)

In our scheme, we do not ask the initiative of our
men. We do not want any initiative. All we want of
them is to obey the orders we give them, do what
we say, and do it quick.

Frederick Winslow Taylor, engineer (1856–1915), *The
Principles of Scientific Management* (1911)

Scientific Management has for its foundation the firm
conviction that the true interests of the two are one
and the same; that prosperity for the employer
cannot exist a long term of years unless it is
accompanied by prosperity for the employee, and
vice versa.

Frederick Winslow Taylor, *The Principles of Scientific
Management* (1911)

The labouring man has not leisure for a true integrity
day by day; he cannot afford to sustain the manliest
relations to men; his labour would be depreciated in

Novel thoughts: five quotes from literature

The secret of great fortunes without apparent cause is a crime forgotten, for it was properly done.

Honoré de Balzac, *Le Père Goriot*

Annual income twenty pounds, annual expenditure nineteen nineteen and six, result happiness. Annual income twenty pounds, annual expenditure twenty pounds nought and six, result misery. The blossom is blighted, the leaf is withered, the god of day goes down upon the dreary scene, and – and in short you are forever floored.

Charles Dickens, *David Copperfield*

I like work: it fascinates me. I can sit and look at it for hours.

Jerome K. Jerome, *Three Men in a Boat*

The public are swine; advertising is the rattling of a stick inside a swill-bucket.

George Orwell, *Keep the Aspidistra Flying*

It is very vulgar to talk about one's business. Only people like stockbrokers do that, and then merely at dinner parties.

Oscar Wilde, *The Importance of Being Earnest*

the market. He has no time to be anything but a machine.

Henry David Thoreau, author (1817–62), *Walden* (1854)

❝ Lawyers and the law

Wrong must not win by technicalities.

Aeschylus, tragedian (c525–455 BC)

Woe unto you also, ye lawyers! for ye lade men with burdens grievous to be borne, and ye yourselves touch not the burdens with one of your fingers.

The Bible, St Luke 11:46

Corporations cannot commit treason, nor be outlawed, nor excommunicated, for they have no souls.

Edward Coke, judge (1552–1634), "The Case of Sutton's Hospital"

I have come to the conclusion that one useless man is called a disgrace; that two are called a law firm; and that three or more become a Congress!

Sherman Edwards, lyricist (1919–81), said by John Adams, a character in *1776* (American musical, 1969)

A verbal contract isn't worth the paper it's written on.

Sam Goldwyn, film producer (1879–1974), attributed (probably erroneously)

A lawyer is a person who writes a 10,000-word document and calls it a "brief".

Franz Kafka, author (1883–1924), attributed

I don't ... want a lawyer to tell me what I cannot do. I hire him to tell me how to do what I want to do.

John Pierpont Morgan, banker (1837–1913)

A lawyer is a man who helps you get what is coming to him.

Laurence Peter, teacher and writer (1919–90)

The first thing we do, let's kill all the lawyers.

William Shakespeare, playwright (1564–1616), Dick the butcher in *Henry VI, Part 2*

As your attorney, it is my duty to inform you that it is not important that you understand what I'm doing or why you're paying me so much money. What's important is that you continue to do so.

Hunter S. Thompson, writer (1937–2005), *Fear and Loathing in Las Vegas* (1972)

Nothing is illegal if a hundred businessmen decide to do it.

Andrew Young, politician (1932–)

❝ Laziness

Among the chief worries of today's business executives is the large number of unemployed still on the payrolls.

Anon

Whenever there is a hard job to be done I assign it to a lazy man; he is sure to find an easy way of doing it.

Walter Chrysler, carmaker (1875–1940)

You can know a person by the kind of desk he keeps. If the president of a company has a clean desk then it must be the executive vice-president who is doing all the work.

Harold Geneen, businessman (1910–97), *Managing* (1984)

This job is all about application. Of the arse to the chair.

Richard Herring, comedian (1967–)

We now say that the Science of Economics, or Business, is the chief concern of humanity. Business is intelligent, useful activity. The word "busy-ness" was coined during the time of Chaucer by certain soldier-aristocrats, men of the leisure class, who prided themselves upon the fact that they did no useful thing. Men of power proved their prowess by holding slaves, and these slaves did all the work. To be idle showed that one was not a slave. But this word "business", first flung in contempt, like Puritan,

Methodist and Quaker, has now become a thing of which to be proud. Idleness is the disgrace, not busy-ness.

Elbert Hubbard, philosopher (1856–1915), *The Philosophy of Elbert Hubbard* (1916)

When we're unemployed, we're called lazy; when the whites are unemployed it's called a depression.

Jesse Jackson, Black rights activist (1941–)

I like work: it fascinates me. I can sit and look at it for hours.

Jerome K. Jerome, novelist (1859–1927), *Three Men in a Boat* (1889)

All of the biggest technological inventions created by man – the airplane, the automobile, the computer – says little about his intelligence, but speaks volumes about his laziness.

Mark Kennedy, politician (1957–)

Doing nothing is very hard to do ... you never know when you're finished.

Leslie Nielsen, comedian (1926–2010)

This common tendency to "take it easy" is greatly increased by bringing a number of men together on similar work and at a uniform standard rate of pay by the day.

Frederick Winslow Taylor, engineer (1856–1915), *The Principles of Scientific Management* (1911)

Work is the curse of the drinking classes.

Oscar Wilde, writer (1854–1900), quoted in *Oscar Wilde, His Life and Confessions* by Frank Harris (1916)

Leadership

He that gives good advice, builds with one hand; he that gives good counsel and example, builds with both; but he that gives good admonition and bad example, builds with one hand and pulls down with the other.

Francis Bacon, philosopher (1561–1626)

Managers do things right. Leaders do the right thing.

Warren Bennis, academic (1925–), *Managing People is Like Herding Cats: Warren Bennis on Leadership* (1999)

A lot of the leaders I've spoken to give expression to their feminine side. Many male leaders are almost bisexual in their ability to be open and reflective.

Warren Bennis

Becoming a leader is synonymous with becoming yourself. It is precisely that simple, and it is also that difficult.

Warren Bennis

The most dangerous leadership myth is that leaders are born – that there is a genetic factor to leadership. This myth asserts that people simply either have certain charismatic qualities or not. That's nonsense; in fact, the opposite is true. Leaders are made rather than born.

Warren Bennis

Example has more followers than reason. We unconsciously imitate what pleases us, and insensibly approximate to the characters we most admire.

Christian Nestell Bovee (1820–1904), *Intuitions and Summaries of Thought* (1862)

Drive thy business or it will drive thee.

Benjamin Franklin, polymath (1705–90)

Questions go unanswered because to address them senior managers must first admit, to themselves and to their employees, that they are less than fully in control of their company's future. So the urgent drives out the important, the future goes largely unexplored; and the capacity to act, rather than the capacity to think and imagine, becomes the sole measure of leadership.

Gary Hamel and **C.K. Prahalad**, management thinkers, *Competing for the Future* (1996)

The very essence of leadership is that you have to have vision. You can't blow an uncertain trumpet.

Theodore Hesburgh, priest (1917–)

A leader must identify himself with the group, must back up the group, even at the risk of displeasing superiors. He must believe that the group wants from him a sense of approval. If this feeling prevails, production, discipline, morale will be high, and in return, you can demand the cooperation to promote the goals of the community.

Vince Lombardi, American football coach (1913–70)

The only way in which anyone can lead you is to restore to you the belief in your own guidance.

Henry Miller, author (1891–1980)

Leadership cannot simply delegate management; instead of distinguishing managers from leaders, we should be seeing managers as leaders, and leadership as management practised well.

Henry Mintzberg, academic (1939–), *Managing* (2009)

It doesn't take a genius to know that every organisation thrives when it has two leaders. Go ahead, name a country that doesn't have two presidents. A boat that sets sail without two captains. Where would Catholicism be without the popes?

Oscar Nunez, character in *The Office* (American TV series)

To loosen the reins, to allow a thousand flowers to bloom and a hundred schools to contend, is the best way to sustain vigour in perilous gyrating times.

Tom Peters, management writer (1942–)

Luck

The right merchant is one who has the just average of faculties we call common sense; a man of a strong affinity for facts, who makes up his decision on what he has seen. He is thoroughly persuaded of the truths of arithmetic. There is always a reason, in the man, for his good or bad fortune in making money. Men talk as if there were some magic about this. He knows that all goes on the old road, pound for pound, cent for cent – for every effect a perfect cause – and that good luck is another name for tenacity of purpose.

Ralph Waldo Emerson, writer (1803–82), *The Conduct of Life* (1860)

Lucky risk takers use hindsight to reinforce their feeling that their gut is very wise. Hindsight also reinforces others' trust in that individual's gut. That's one of the real dangers of leader selection in many organisations: leaders are selected for overconfidence. We associate leadership with decisiveness.

Daniel Kahneman, psychologist (1934–), *McKinsey Quarterly*, May 2008

Luck is what happens when preparation meets opportunity.

Seneca, philosopher (4BC–65AD)

When you are employed, hence dependent on other people's judgement, looking busy can help you claim responsibility for the results in a random environment. The appearance of busyness reinforces the perception of causality, of the link between results and one's role in them.

Nassim Nicholas Taleb, writer (1960–), *The Black Swan: The Impact of the Highly Improbable* (2007)

M

66 Management speak and jargon

What I need is a list of specific unknown problems
we will encounter.

Anon memo to staff at a shipping company

I hear managers at the bank [say] "let's touch base
about that offline". I think it means have a private
chat but I am still not sure.

Anon, 50 worst examples of management speak, BBC

There's no "I" in "team". But then there's no "I" in
"useless smug colleague", either. And there's four in
"platitude-quoting idiot".

Anon

I cannot speak well enough to be unintelligible.

Jane Austen, author (1775–1817), *Northanger Abbey*

What differentiates a business thought from a
normal thought is that business thoughts have a
"going forward" at the end of them going forward.
It's also vital that you know that for the envelope to
be pushed out of the box and through the window

of opportunity, customers should first become stakeholders and then delighted beyond their expectations. In order to do this, top executives will go forward the extra mile while wearing the shoes of the customer. And remember, the customer is king (unless she is a woman).

Guy Browning, humorist (1964–), *Office Politics: How Work Really Works* (2006)

If one cannot state a matter clearly enough so that even an intelligent 12-year-old can understand it, one should remain within the cloistered walls of the university and laboratory until one gets a better grasp of one's subject matter.

Margaret Mead, anthropologist (1901–78)

Staff who work for big corporate organisations find themselves using management speak as a way of disguising the fact that they haven't done their job properly. Some people think that it is easy to bluff their way through by using long, impressive-sounding words and phrases, even if they don't know what they mean.

Report by the Plain English Campaign

You and I come by road, or rail, but economists travel on infrastructure.

Margaret Thatcher, British prime minister (1925–)

❝ Management thinking

Business has continued to be more interested in thinking, in general, than any other sector of society. The explanation for this is because there is a reality test. There is a bottom line. There are sales figures and profit figures. There are results.

Edward de Bono, consultant (1933–), Management-Issues. com, June 2010

For people in any position of authority the ability to say no is the most important skill there is ... No, you can't have a pay rise. No, you can't be promoted. No, you can't travel club class. No, we are not going to an offsite workshop to discuss living our core values ... An illogical love of Yes is the basis for all modern management thought. The ideal modern manager is meant to be enabling, empowering, encouraging and nurturing, which means that his default position must be Yes. By contrast, No is considered demotivating, uncreative and a thoroughly bad thing.

Lucy Kellaway, writer (1959–), *Financial Times*, July 2007

❝ Managers and management

The only managers that have simple problems have simple minds.

Russell Ackoff, academic (1919–2009)

Words from the wise: five quotes from management gurus

There is only one definition of business purpose: to create a customer.

Peter Drucker

Good companies will meet needs. Great companies will create markets.

Philip Kotler

People don't want quarter-inch drills. They want quarter-inch holes.

Theodore Levitt

There is no such thing as a minor lapse of integrity.

Tom Peters

If your aspirations are not greater than your resources, you're not an entrepreneur.

C.K. Prahalad

Failing organisations are usually over-managed and under-led.

Warren Bennis, academic (1925–), "Why lead?", *Executive Excellence* (2006)

If you can run one business well, you can run any business well.

Richard Branson, founder of Virgin (1950–)

People join companies but leave managers.

Marcus Buckingham and **Curt Coffman**, *First, Break All the Rules* (1999)

The task is to manage what there is and to work to create what could and should be.

Peter Drucker, management writer (1909–2005), *Managing in Turbulent Times* (1980)

Management is so much more than exercising rank and privilege ... it is much more than "making deals". Management affects people and their lives.

Peter Drucker, *Managing in a Time of Great Change* (1995)

Management is about human beings. Its task is to make people capable of joint performance, to make their strengths effective and their weaknesses irrelevant.

Peter Drucker, *The Profession of Management* (1998)

The man who always knows how will always have a job. The man who also knows why will always be his boss.

Ralph Waldo Emerson, writer (1803–82)

Management: an activity or art where those who have not yet succeeded and those who have proved

unsuccessful are led by those who have not yet
failed.

Paulsson Frenckner, economist (1929–2005)

Management was designed to solve a very specific
problem – how to do things with perfect replicability,
at ever-increasing scale and steadily increasing
efficiency. Now there's a new set of challenges on
the horizon. How do you build organisations that are
as nimble as change itself? How do you mobilise
and monetise the imagination of every employee,
every day? How do you create organisations that are
highly engaging places to work in? And these
challenges simply can't be met without reinventing
our 100-year-old management model.

Gary Hamel, management thinker (1954–), *McKinsey
Quarterly*, November 2007

Management cannot provide a man with self-respect,
or with the respect of his fellows, or with the
satisfaction of needs for self-fulfilment. We can create
the conditions such that he is encouraged and
enabled to seek such satisfactions for himself, or we
can thwart him by failing to create those conditions.

Douglas McGregor, academic (1906–64), *The Human Side of
Enterprise* (1960)

The pressures of his job drive the manager to be
superficial in his actions – to overload himself with
work, encourage interruption, respond quickly to
every stimulus, seek the tangible and avoid the

abstract, make decisions in small increments, and do everything abruptly.

Henry Mintzberg, academic (1939–), "The Manager's Job: Folklore and Fact", *Harvard Business Review*, 1975

The effective managers seem to be not those with the greatest degrees of freedom but the ones who use to advantage whatever degrees of freedom they can find.

Henry Mintzberg, *Mintzberg on Management* (1989)

A good manager acts at two extremes of scale – the most general values, the most specific details – and leaves it to workers to engage the middle ground as they see fit.

Michael Preis, academic, *101 Things I Learned In Business School* (2010)

The best executive is the one who has sense enough to pick good men to do what he wants done, and self-restraint to keep from meddling with them while they do it.

Theodore Roosevelt, American president (1858–1919)

I swore to myself that if I ever got to walk around the room as manager, people would laugh when they saw me coming and would applaud as I walked away.

Michael Scott, character in *The Office* (American TV series)

❝ Manufacturing

The merchant's function (or manufacturer's, for in the broad sense in which it is here used the word must be understood to include both) is to provide for the nation. It is no more his function to get profit for himself out of that provision than it is a clergyman's function to get his stipend.

John Ruskin, critic (1819–1900), "The Roots of Honour" in *Unto This Last* (1862)

The great cry that rises from our manufacturing cities, louder than their furnace blast, is all in very deed for this – that we manufacture everything there except men; we blanch cotton, and strengthen steel, and refine sugar, and shape pottery; but to brighten, to strengthen, to refine, or to form a single living spirit, never enters into our estimate of advantages.

John Ruskin, *The Stones of Venice* (1871–53)

❝ Market research

Some people use research like a drunkard uses a lamppost: for support, not illumination.

David Ogilvy, advertising executive (1911–99), quoted in *New York* magazine, August 1983

Running a company on market research is like driving while looking in the rear view mirror.

Anita Roddick, businesswoman (1942–2007), quoted in the *Independent*, August 1997

Focus groups are a waste of time, filled with people telling you what you want to hear so they can go home.

Sergio Zymen, marketing executive (1945–)

66 Marketing

The only way on earth to influence other people is to talk about what they want and show them how to get it.

Dale Carnegie, writer (1888–1955), *How to Win Friends and Influence People* (1936)

No one likes to feel that he or she is being sold something or told to do a thing. We much prefer to feel that we are buying of our own accord or acting on our own ideas. We like to be consulted about our wishes, our wants, our thoughts.

Dale Carnegie, *How to Win Friends and Influence People* (1936)

You can close more business in two months by becoming interested in other people than you can in two years by trying to get people interested in you.

Dale Carnegie, *How to Win Friends and Influence People* (1936)

"Marketing" has become a fashionable term. But a gravedigger remains a gravedigger even when called a "mortician"--only the cost of burial goes up.'

Peter Drucker, management writer (1909–2005), *Managing for Results* (1964)

The aim of marketing is to make selling superfluous.

Peter Drucker, *Management, Tasks, Responsibilities, Practices* (1973)

We believe what we want to believe, and once we believe something, it becomes a self-fulfilling truth.

Seth Godin, entrepreneur (1960–), *All Marketers Are Liars* (2005)

Don't try to change someone's worldview is the strategy smart marketers follow. Don't try to use facts to prove your case and to insist that people change their biases. You don't have enough time and you don't have enough money. Instead, identify a population with a certain worldview, frame your story in terms of that worldview and you win.

Seth Godin, *All Marketers Are Liars* (2005)

Marketing is about spreading ideas, and spreading ideas is the single most important output of our civilisation.

Seth Godin, *All Marketers Are Liars* (2005)

It's easy to assume people are conforming when we witness them all choosing the same option, but when we choose that very option ourselves, we have no shortage of perfectly good reasons for why we just happen to be doing the same thing as those other people; they mindlessly conform, but we mindfully choose ... Rather than being alone in a crowd of sheep, we're all individuals in sheep's clothing.

Sheena Iyengar, academic (1969–), *The Art of Choosing* (2010)

Marketing is not the art of finding clever ways to dispose of what you make. Marketing is the art of creating genuine customer value. It is the art of helping your customers become better off.

Philip Kotler, academic (1931–), *Marketing Insights from A to Z: 80 Concepts Every Manager Needs to Know* (2003)

Authentic marketing is not the art of selling what you make but knowing what to make.

Philip Kotler, academic (1931–), *Marketing Management* (first published 1967)

Business has only two functions – marketing and innovation.

Milan Kundera, author (1929–)

In the modern world of business, it is useless to be a creative original thinker unless you can also sell what you create. Management cannot be expected to recognise a good idea unless it is presented to them by a good salesman.

David Ogilvy, advertising executive (1911–99), *Confessions of an Advertising Man* (1961)

Marketing is not a battle of products, it's a battle of perceptions.

Al Ries and **Jack Trout**, *The 22 Immutable Laws Of Marketing* (1994)

I do not believe in censorship, but I believe we already have censorship in what is called marketing theory, namely the only information we get in mainstream media is for profit.

Sam Shepard, film director (1943–)

Advertising is not an art form. The sole purpose of marketing is to sell more stuff more often to more people for more money.

Sergio Zymen, marketing executive (1945–), *The End of Marketing as We Know It* (1999)

66 Markets

I'd be a bum on the street with a tin cup if the markets were always efficient.

Warren Buffett, investor (1930–), quoted in *Fortune*, April 1995

With some notable exceptions, businessmen favour free enterprise in general but are opposed to it when it comes to themselves.

Milton Friedman, economist (1912–2006), lecture, 1983

The market can stay irrational longer than you can stay solvent.

John Maynard Keynes, economist (1883–1946)

Good companies will meet needs. Great companies will create markets.

Philip Kotler, academic (1931–), *Marketing Management* (first published 1967)

In the long run, every market becomes a two horse race.

Al Ries and **Jack Trout**, *The 22 Immutable Laws Of Marketing* (1994)

❝ The media

The press is the hired agent of a monied system, and set up for no other purpose than to tell lies where their interests are involved.

Henry Adams, writer (1838–1918), *The Letters of Henry Adams* (1882)

With all the mass media concentrated in a few hands, the ancient faith in the competition of ideas in the free market seems like a hollow echo of a much simpler day.

Kingman Brewster junior, academic and diplomat (1919–88)

Burke said there were Three Estates in Parliament; but, in the Reporters' Gallery yonder, there sat a Fourth Estate more important far than they all.

Thomas Carlyle, historian (1795–1881), quoting Edmund Burke in *On Heroes and Hero Worship* (1841)

Freedom of the press in Britain is freedom to print such of the proprietor's prejudices as the advertisers won't object to.

Helen Swaffer

The TV business is uglier than most things. It is normally perceived as some kind of cruel and shallow money trench through the heart of the journalism industry, a long plastic hallway where thieves and pimps run free and good men die like dogs, for no good reason.

Hunter S. Thompson, writer (1937–2005), *Gonzo Papers, Vol. 2* (1988)

The fact is that the public have an insatiable curiosity to know everything. Except what is worth knowing. Journalism, conscious of this, and having tradesman-like habits, supplies their demands.

Oscar Wilde, writer (1854–1900), *The Soul of Man Under Socialism* (1891)

The media's the most powerful entity on earth. They have the power to make the innocent guilty and to make the guilty innocent, and that's power. Because they control the minds of the masses.

Malcolm X, Black rights activist (1925–65)

❝ Meetings

Here's my theory about meetings and life; the three things you can't fake are erections, competence and creativity. That's why meetings become toxic – they put uncreative people in a situation in which they have to be something they can never be. And the more effort they put into concealing their inabilities, the more toxic the meeting becomes. One of the most common creativity-faking tactics is when someone puts their hands in prayer position and conceals their mouth while they nod at you and say, "Mmmmmm. Interesting". If pressed, they'll add, "I'll have to get back to you on that." Then they don't say anything else.

Douglas Coupland, author (1961–), *JPod* (2006)

Always hold your sales meetings in rooms too small for the audience, even if it means holding them in the WC. "Standing room only" creates an atmosphere of success, as in theatres and restaurants, while a half-empty auditorium smells of failure.

David Ogilvy, advertising executive (1911–99), *Ogilvy on Advertising* (1983)

People who enjoy meetings should not be in charge of anything.

Thomas Sowell, economist (1930–), *Ever Wonder Why? and Other Controversial Essays* (2006)

Mergers, demergers and acquisitions

The big danger in mega-mergers is that they are seen as a mating of dinosaurs.

Peter Bonfield, businessman (1944–), quoted in the *Sunday Times*, July 2000

Of one thing be certain: if a CEO is enthused about a particularly foolish acquisition, both his internal staff and his outside advisers will come up with whatever projections are needed to justify his stance. Only in fairy tales are emperors told that they are naked.

Warren Buffett, investor (1930–)

Chief executives seem no more able to resist their biological urge to merge, than dogs can resist chasing rabbits.

Philip Coggan, writer (1959–), quoted in *Dean LeBaron's Treasury of Investment Wisdom* (2001)

Much of what is called investment is actually nothing more than mergers and acquisitions, and of course mergers and acquisitions are generally accompanied by downsizing.

Susan George, political scientist (1934–)

You might merge with another organisation, but two drunks don't make a sensible person.

Gary Hamel and **C.K. Prahalad**, management thinkers, *Competing for the Future* (1996)

I always said that mega-mergers were for megalomaniacs.

David Ogilvy, advertising executive (1911–1999)

Dividing an elephant in half does not produce two elephants.

Peter Senge, scientist (1947–), *The Fifth Discipline: The Art and Practice of The Learning Organization* (1990)

When it comes to mergers, hope triumphs over experience.

Irwin Stelzer, economist (1932–)

66 Money

Money is a terrible master but an excellent servant.

P.T. Barnum, showman (1810–91)

No one can serve two masters. For you will hate one and love the other; you will be devoted to one and despise the other. You cannot serve both God and money.

The Bible, Matthew 6:24

The happiest time in a man's life is when he is in the red hot pursuit of a dollar with a reasonable prospect of overtaking it.

Josh Billings, humorist (1818–85)

Business is a good game – lots of competition and a minimum of rules. You keep score with money.

Nolan Bushnell, founder of Atari (1943–)

It is a kind of spiritual snobbery that makes people think they can be happy without money.

Albert Camus, author (1913–60)

Money doesn't talk, it swears.

Bob Dylan, musician (1941–), *It's Alright Ma (I'm Only Bleeding)*

Money is not the maiden's virtue, it's the currency of whores.

John Gaherin, attorney (1914–2000)

What's worth doing is worth doing for money.

Gordon Gekko, character in *Wall Street* (feature film, 1987)

The love of money as a possession – as distinguished from the love of money as a means to the enjoyments and realities of life – will be recognised for what it is, a somewhat disgusting morbidity, one of those semi-criminal, semi-pathological

propensities which one hands over with a shudder
to the specialists in mental disease.

John Maynard Keynes, economist (1883–1946), "The Future",
Essays in Persuasion (1923)

The chief value of money lies in the fact that one
lives in a world in which is it is overestimated.

H.L. Mencken, writer (1880–1956), *A Mencken Chrestomathy*
(1916)

If a man is after money, he's money mad; if he keeps
it, he's a capitalist; if he spends it, he's a playboy; if
he doesn't get it, he's a never-do-well; if he doesn't
try to get it, he lacks ambition. If he gets it without
working for it, he's a parasite; and if he accumulates
it after a lifetime of hard work, people call him a fool
who never got anything out of life.

Vic Oliver, comedian (1898–1964)

So you think that money is the root of all evil? Have
you ever asked what is the root of money? Money is
a tool of exchange, which can't exist unless there are
goods produced and men able to produce them.
Money is the material shape of the principle that
men who wish to deal with one another must deal
by trade and give value for value. Money is not the
tool of the moochers, who claim your product by
tears, or of the looters, who take it from you by force.
Money is made possible only by the men who
produce. Is this what you consider evil?

Ayn Rand, author (1905–82), *Atlas Shrugged* (1957)

I know of nothing more despicable and pathetic than a man who devotes all the hours of the waking day to the making of money for money's sake.

John D. Rockefeller, industrialist (1839–1937)

It is not the creation of wealth that is wrong, but the love of money for its own sake.

Margaret Thatcher, British prime minister (1925–)

No one would remember the Good Samaritan if he'd only had good intentions; he had money as well.

Margaret Thatcher

When a fellow says it ain't the money but the principle of the thing, it's the money.

Artemus Ward, humorist (1834–67)

❝ Motivation

If you think you can do a thing or think you can't do a thing, you're right.

Henry Ford, industrialist (1863–1947)

A man generally has two reasons for doing a thing. One that sounds good, and a real one.

John Pierpont Morgan, banker (1837–1913)

❝ The music industry

We live in an age of music for people who don't like music. The record industry discovered some time ago that there aren't that many people who actually like music. For a lot of people, music's annoying, or at the very least they don't need it. They discovered if they could sell music to a lot of those people, they could sell a lot more records.

T-Bone Burnett, musician (1948–)

A group or an artist shouldn't get his money until his boss gets his.

Bobby Darin, musician (1936–73), quoted in *Bobby Darin: The Incredible Story of an Amazing Life* by Al DiOrio (2004)

The music business can be very cold. And it doesn't honour its elders.

Brenda Lee, musician (1944–)

There are two kinds of artists left: those who endorse Pepsi and those who simply won't.

Annie Lennox, musician (1954–)

A woman's two cents worth is worth two cents in the music business.

Loretta Lynn, musician (1935–)

You know, the music business is like the Lotto. Just put your numbers down and sometimes they hit, and sometimes they don't.

Barry McGuire, musician (1965–)

Music is spiritual. The music business is not.

Van Morrison, musician (1945–)

At the record company meeting
On their hands – at last! – a dead star

Morrissey, musician (1959–), *Paint a Vulgar Picture*

I'm not a businessman. I'm a business, man.

Jay-Z, musician (1969–), *Diamonds*

Modern music is people who can't think signing artists who can't write songs to make records for people who can't hear.

Frank Zappa, musician (1940–93)

N

66 Negotiation and dealmaking

Here's the rule for bargains. "Do other men, for they would do you." That's the true business precept.
Charles Dickens, novelist (1812–70), *Martin Chuzzlewit* (1843–44)

The man who is willing to meet you halfway is usually a poor judge of distance.
Laurence Peter, teacher and writer (1919–90)

I'll give thrice so much land
To any well-deserving friend;
But in the way of bargain, mark ye me,
I'll cavil on the ninth part of a hair.
William Shakespeare, playwright (1564–1616), Hotspur in *Henry IV Part I*

Deals are my art form. Other people paint beautifully on canvas or write wonderful poetry. I like making deals, preferably big deals.
Donald Trump, businessman (1946–), *New York* magazine, November 1987

O

‟ Obsession

Executives are like joggers. If you stop a jogger, he
goes on running on the spot. If you drag an executive
away from his business, he goes on running on the
spot, pawing the ground, talking business. He never
stops hurtling onwards, making decisions and
executing them.

Jean Baudrillard, sociologist (1929–2007), *Cool Memories*
(1987)

I do not believe a man can ever leave his business.
He ought to think of it by day and dream of it by
night.

Henry Ford, industrialist (1863–1947)

‟ Obstacles

There are no big problems, there are just a lot of little
problems.

Henry Ford, industrialist (1863–1947)

Man is most uniquely human when he turns obstacles into opportunities.

Eric Hoffer, philosopher (1902–83), *Between the Devil and the Dragon* (1982)

No problem can be solved until it is reduced to some simple form. The changing of a vague difficulty into a specific, concrete form is a very essential element in thinking.

John Pierpont Morgan, banker (1837–1913)

Things are only impossible until they are not.

Jean-Luc Picard, commander of the *Starship Enterprise*

For every complex problem there is a simple solution that is wrong.

George Bernard Shaw, playwright (1856–1950)

Success is to be measured not so much by the position that one has reached in life as by the obstacles which have been overcome while trying to succeed.

Booker T. Washington, teacher (1856–1915)

❝ Office life

In an open plan office there is a ritual where everyone waits hours for the first person to say: "Who wants a coffee?" That person then finds themselves in the kitchen for the rest of the day working as a junior catering manager.

Guy Browning, humorist (1964–), *Office Politics: How Work Really Works* (2006)

It's an absolute rule that the person who earns least in the office will be the first person to buy a round after work. He is also the first to get absolutely hammered and say something so offensive that he gets passed over for a raise for the seventh year running.

Guy Browning, *Office Politics: How Work Really Works* (2006)

The people you work with are people you were just thrown together with. I mean, you don't know them, it wasn't your choice. And yet you spend more time with them than you do your friends or your family. But probably all you have in common is the fact that you walk around on the same bit of carpet for eight hours a day.

Tim Canterbury, character in *The Office* (British TV series, 2003)

Oh, you hate your job? Why didn't you say so? There's a support group for that. It's called everybody, and they meet at the bar.

Drew Carey, comedian (1958–)

When you grow up you'll be put in a container called a cubicle. The bleak oppressiveness will warp your spine and destroy your capacity to feel joy.

Luckily you'll have a boss like me to motivate you with something called fear.

Dilbert comic strip

To make a long story short, there's nothing like having a boss walk in.

Doris Lilly, author (1922–91)

Work is the curse of the drinking classes.

Oscar Wilde, writer (1854–1900), quoted in *Oscar Wilde, His Life and Confessions* by Frank Harris (1916)

66 The oil and gas industry

Omnia bona quoad perfora (All prospects look good until drilled)

Motto of Anardoko Petroleum Corporation

Courage, determination, and hard work are all very nice, but not so nice as an oil well in the back yard.

Mason Cooley, aphorist (1927–2002), *City Aphorisms*

We usually find gas in new places with old ideas. Sometimes, also, we find gas in an old place with a new idea, but we seldom find much gas in an old place with an old idea. Several times in the past we have thought that we were running out of gas, whereas actually we were only running out of ideas.

Parke Dickey, geologist (1909–95), quoted in *Encyclopaedia of Petroleum Science and Engineering*

We are like tenant farmers chopping down the fence around our house for fuel when we should be using Nature's inexhaustible sources of energy – sun, wind and tide. I'd put my money on the sun and solar energy. What a source of power! I hope we don't have to wait until oil and coal run out before we tackle that.

Thomas Edison, inventor (1847–1931)

First rule of oil – addicts never tell the truth to their pushers. We are the addicts, the oil producers are the pushers – we've never had an honest conversation with the Saudis.

Thomas Friedman, writer (1953–)

My formula for success? Rise early, work late, strike oil.

Jean Paul Getty, oil magnate (1892–1976), *As I See It* (1976)

Let me tell you something that we Israelis have against Moses. He took us 40 years through the desert in order to bring us to the one spot in the Middle East that has no oil.

Golda Meir, Israeli prime minister (1898–1978), quoted in the *New York Times*, June 1973

The use of solar energy has not been opened up because the oil industry does not own the sun.

Ralph Nadar, activist (1934–)

Gold is where you find it, according to an old adage, but judging from the record of our experience, oil must be sought first of all in our minds.

Wallace Pratt, geologist, (1885–1981), *Oil in the Earth* (1944)

Oil prices have fallen lately. We include this news for the benefit of gas stations, which otherwise wouldn't learn of it for six months.

William Tammeus, writer, *The Globe and Mail* (Toronto), 1991

❝ The oldest profession

The profession of a prostitute is the only career in which the maximum income is paid to the newest apprentice. It is the one calling in which at the beginning the only exertion is that of self-indulgence; all the prizes are at the commencement. It is the ever-new embodiment of the old fable of the sale of the soul to the Devil. The tempter offers wealth, comfort, excitement, but in return the victim must sell her soul, nor does the other party forget to exact his due to the uttermost farthing.

Charles Booth, philanthropist (1840–1916)

Prostitution is the supreme triumph of capitalism. Worst of all, prostitution reinforces all the old dumb clichés about women's sexuality; that they are not built to enjoy sex and are little more than walking masturbation aids, things to be DONE TO, things so sensually null and void that they have to be paid to indulge in fornication, that women can be had, bought, as often as not sold from one man to another. When the sex war is won prostitutes should be shot as collaborators for their terrible betrayal of all women, for the moral tarring and feathering they give indigenous women who have had the bad luck to live in what they make their humping ground.

Julie Burchill, writer (1959–)

If my business was legitimate, I would deduct a substantial percentage for depreciation of my body.

Xaviera Holland, call girl (1943–), *The Happy Hooker* (1971)

We say that slavery has vanished from European civilisation, but this is not true. Slavery still exists, but now it applies only to women and its name is prostitution.

Victor Hugo, writer (1802–85), *Les Misérables* (1862)

66 Operations

There is nothing more requisite in business than dispatch.

Joseph Addison, essayist and playwright (1672–1719), *The Drummer* (1716)

❝ Optimism

Pessimists are usually right and optimists are usually wrong but all the great changes have been accomplished by optimists.

Thomas Friedman, writer (1953–), *The World Is Flat: A Brief History of the Twenty-First Century* (2005)

One of the major biases in risky decision making is optimism.

Daniel Kahneman, psychologist (1934–), *McKinsey Quarterly*, May 2008

P

66 Performance

It is much more difficult to measure non-performance than performance. Performance stands out like a ton of diamonds. Non-performance can almost always be explained away.
Harold Geneen, businessman (1910–97)

It is an immutable law in business that words are words, explanations are explanations, promises are promises – but only performance is reality.
Harold Geneen

66 Philanthropy

Let the business of the world take care of itself ... My business is to get the world saved; if this involves the standing still of the looms and the shutting up of the factories, and the staying of the sailing of the ships, let them all stand still. When we have got everybody converted they can go on again, and we shall be able to keep things going then by working half time and

have the rest to spend in loving one another and
worshipping God.

William Booth, founder of the Salvation Army (1829–1912),
The War Cry, December 1884

Philosophy

A man of business may talk of philosophy; a man
who has none may practise it.

Alexander Pope, poet (1688–1744), *Thoughts on Various
Subjects* (1727)

Improve yourself: that is the only thing you can to
improve the world.

Ludwig Wittgenstein, philosopher (1889–1951)

Planning

Prediction is very difficult. Especially about the
future.

Niels Bohr, scientist (1885–1962), attributed

Measure twice, cut once.

Carpenters' mantra

Planning is an unnatural process; it is much more fun
to do something. And the nicest thing about not
planning is that failure comes as a complete surprise

rather than being preceded by a period of worry and depression.

John Harvey Jones, businessman (1924–2008)

A goal properly set is halfway reached.

Abraham Lincoln, American president (1809–65)

A stockbroker urged me to buy a stock that would triple in value every year. I told him: "At my age I don't even buy green bananas."

Claude Pepper, politician (1900–89)

66 Poverty

I've always been after the trappings of great luxury. But all I've got hold of are the trappings of great poverty. I've got hold of the wrong load of trappings, and a rotten load they are too, ones I could have very well done without.

Peter Cook, satirist (1937–95), *Beyond the Fringe* (British satirical revue, 1960s)

To be idle and to be poor have always been reproaches, and therefore every man endeavours with his utmost care to hide his poverty from others, and his idleness from himself.

Samuel Johnson, author (1709–84)

If we stop thinking of the poor as victims or as a burden and start recognising them as resilient and creative entrepreneurs and value-conscious consumers, a whole new world of opportunity will open up.

C.K. Prahalad, academic (1941–2010), *The Fortune at the Bottom of the Pyramid* (2004)

Power

Power is America's last dirty word. It is easier to talk about money – and much easier to talk about sex – than it is to talk about power. People who have it deny it; people who want it do not want to appear to hunger for it; and people who engage in its machinations do so secretly.

Rosabeth Moss Kanter, academic (1943–), "Power Failure in Management Circuits", *Harvard Business Review*, July 1979

The powerless live in a different world. Lacking the supplies, information, or support to make things happen easily, they may turn instead to the ultimate weapon of those who lack productive power – oppressive power: holding others back and punishing with whatever threats they can muster.

Rosabeth Moss Kanter, "Power Failure in Management Circuits", *Harvard Business Review*, July 1979

[Within firms there are] islands of conscious power in this ocean of unconscious co-operation like lumps of butter coagulating in a pail of buttermilk.

Dennis Holme Robertson, economist (1890–1963), quoted in *The Nature of the Firm* by Ronald Coase (1937)

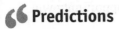 Predictions

Saudi Arabia appears devoid of all prospects for oil.
Attributed to a director of Anglo Persian Oil Company in 1926

Stocks have reached what seems like a permanently high plateau.
Irving Fisher, economist (1867–1947), speaking three days before the 1929 stockmarket crash

You young folks remember, IBM was built on punch cards, and our foundation will always be punch cards.
IBM executive, on the development of a tape drive around 1940, quoted in *The Economist*, June 2011

This "telephone" has too many shortcomings to be seriously considered as a means of communication. The device is inherently of no value to us.
Western Union memo, 1876

Price

There are two kinds of companies, those that work to try to charge more and those that work to charge less. We will be the second.
Jeff Bezos, founder of Amazon (1964–)

There is no victory at bargain basement prices.
Dwight D. Eisenhower, American president (1890–1969), speech to troops before the Normandy landings

If you have to ask how much it costs, you can't afford it.

John Pierpont Morgan, banker (1837–1913)

Prices are important not because money is considered paramount but because prices are a fast and effective conveyor of information through a vast society in which fragmented knowledge must be co-ordinated.

Thomas Sowell, economist (1930–), *Knowledge and Decisions* (1980)

❝ Procrastination

I love deadlines. I like the whooshing sound they make as they fly by.

Douglas Adams, author (1952–2001)

We are all manufacturers. Making good, making trouble, or making excuses.

H.V. Adolt

Without action, the world would still be an idea.

George Doriot, founder of INSEAD business school (1899–1987)

Even a correct decision is wrong when it was taken too late.

Lee Iacocca, businessman (1924–)

Work expands to fill the time available for its completion.

Cyril Northcote Parkinson, historian (1909–93), *Parkinson's Law* (1957)

A good solution applied with vigour now is better than a perfect solution applied ten minutes later.

George Patton, American general (1885–1945), quoted in *The Unknown Patton* (1983) by Charles M. Province

Products

Quality in a product or service is not what the supplier puts in. It is what the customer gets out and is willing to pay for. A product is not quality because it is hard to make and costs a lot of money, as manufacturers typically believe. This is incompetence. Customers pay only for what is of use to them and gives them value. Nothing else constitutes quality.

Peter Drucker, management writer (1909–2005), *Innovation and Entrepreneurship* (1985)

A market is never saturated with a good product, but it is very quickly saturated with a bad one.

Henry Ford, industrialist (1863–1947)

Designing your product for monetisation first, and people second will probably leave you with neither.

Tara Hunt, businesswoman (1973–)

The despatch box: five quotes from politicians

The inherent vice of capitalism is the uneven division of blessings, while the inherent virtue of socialism is the equal division of misery.

Winston Churchill

The chief business of the America people is business.

Calvin Coolidge

Let me tell you something that we Israelis have against Moses. He took us 40 years through the desert in order to bring us to the one spot in the Middle East that has no oil.

Golda Meir

The best executive is the one who has sense enough to pick good men to do what he wants done, and self-restraint to keep from meddling with them while they do it.

Theodore Roosevelt

Socialist governments traditionally do make a financial mess. They always run out of other people's money. It's quite a characteristic of them.

Margaret Thatcher

Never let an inventor run a company. You can never get him to stop tinkering and bring something to market.

Royal Little, businessman (1896–1989)

❝ Progress

The merchant goes home after a day of hard work and excitement to a late dinner, trying amid the family circle to forget business, when he is interrupted by a telegram from London ... and the poor man must dispatch his dinner as hurriedly as possible in order to send his message to California. The businessman of the present day must be continually on the jump, the slow express train will not answer his purpose, and the poor merchant has no other way in which to work to secure a living for his family. He must use the telegraph.

W.E. Dodge, businessman (1805–83)

Restlessness is discontent – and discontent is the first necessity of progress. Show me a thoroughly satisfied man – and I will show you a failure.

Thomas Edison, inventor (1847–1931)

Progress is what happens when impossibility yields to necessity.

Arnold H. Glasow, humorist (1905–98)

Those who do not industrialise become hewers of wood and haulers of water.

Alexander Hamilton, statesman (1755–1894)

One withstands the invasion of armies; one does not withstand the invasion of ideas.

Victor Hugo, writer (1802–85), *The History of a Crime* (1877)

As far as I'm concerned, progress peaked with frozen pizza.

John McClane, character in *Die Hard 2* (feature film, 1990)

Do not confuse motion and progress. A rocking horse keeps moving but does not make any progress.

Alfred Montapert, author

The reasonable man adapts himself to the world; the unreasonable one persists in trying to adapt the world to himself. Therefore, all progress depends on the unreasonable man.

George Bernard Shaw, playwright (1856–1950), *Maxims for Revolutionists* (1903)

Lo! Men have become the tools of their tools.

Henry David Thoreau, author (1817–62), *Walden* (1854)

❝ Promotion

You would think that lazy people would form an inert mass at the bottom of an organisation. On the contrary they are found at all levels in business, right up to chair person. The reason for this is simple: when something goes wrong in business it's generally because someone somewhere has tried to do something. Obviously, if you don't do anything, you can't be blamed when it goes wrong. People who sit all day like a lemon, busily straightening paperclips, are therefore the only people with a 100% record of success, and with that sort of record, promotion is inevitable.

Guy Browning, humorist (1964–), *Office Politics: How Work Really Works* (2006)

In a hierarchy, every employee tends to rise to the level of his incompetence.

Laurence Peter, teacher and writer (1919–90), *The Peter Principle* (with Raymond Hull, 1969)

❝ Purpose

The business of business is business.

Alfred Sloan, industrialist (1875–1966)

R

66 Regulation

If ... a government refrains from regulations and allows matters to take their course, essential commodities soon attain a level of price out of the reach of all but the rich, the worthlessness of the money becomes apparent, and the fraud upon the public can be concealed no longer.

John Maynard Keynes, economist (1883–1946), *The Economic Consequences of the Peace* (1919)

People of the same trade seldom meet together, even for merriment and diversion, but the conversation ends in a conspiracy against the public, or in some contrivance to raise prices. It is impossible indeed to prevent such meetings, by any law which either could be executed, or would be consistent with liberty or justice. But though the law cannot hinder people of the same trade from sometimes assembling together, it ought to do nothing to facilitate such assemblies; much less to render them necessary.

Adam Smith, economist (1723–90), *An Inquiry into the Nature and Causes of the Wealth of Nations* (1776)

It is the highest impertinence and presumption, therefore, in kings and ministers, to pretend to watch over the economy of private people, and to restrain their expence, either by sumptuary laws, or by prohibiting the importation of foreign luxuries. They are themselves always, and without any exception, the greatest spendthrifts in the society. Let them look well after their own expence, and they may safely trust private people with theirs. If their own extravagance does not ruin the state, that of their subjects never will.

Adam Smith, *An Inquiry into the Nature and Causes of the Wealth of Nations* (1776)

❝ Remuneration

All I've ever wanted was an honest week's pay for an honest day's work.

Sergeant Ernest Bilko, character in *Sergeant Bilko* (feature film, 1996)

"A fair day's wages for a fair day's work": it is as just a demand as governed men ever made of governing. It is the everlasting right of man.

Thomas Carlyle, historian (1795–1881), *Past and Present* (1843)

In the general course of human nature, a power over a man's subsistence amounts to a power over his will.

Alexander Hamilton, statesman (1755–1804), *The Federalist Papers* (1787–88)

We pretend to work and they pretend to pay us!

Soviet-era joke

Senior management's job is to pay people. If they fuck a hundred guys out of a hundred grand each, that's ten million more for them. They have four categories: happy, satisfied, dissatisfied, disgusted. If they hit happy, they've screwed up: they never want you happy. On the other hand, they don't want you so disgusted you quit. The sweet spot is somewhere between dissatisfied and disgusted.

Greg Lippman, banker, quoted in *The Big Short* by Michael Lewis (2010)

I like "cheque" and "enclosed".

Dorothy Parker, writer (1893–1967), on being asked the most beautiful words in the English language; quoted in the *New York Herald Tribune*, 1932

The highest reward for a person's toil is not what they get for it, but what they become by it.

John Ruskin, critic (1819–1900)

Currencies fluctuate; commodity prices fluctuate. Why should we expect earnings to rise in a straight line upward?

William Shenkir, academic

The real minimum wage is zero.

Thomas Sowell, economist (1930–), *Controversial Essays* (2002)

Reputation

A man is known by the company he organises.

Ambrose Bierce, satirist (1842–1914), *The Devil's Dictionary* (1911)

It takes 20 years to build a reputation and five minutes to ruin it. If you think about that, you'll do things differently.

Warren Buffett, investor (1930–)

Would you rather be the world's greatest lover, but have everyone think you're the world's worst lover? Or would you rather be the world's worst lover but have everyone think you're the world's greatest lover? Now, that's an interesting question.

Warren Buffett

There are two modes of establishing our reputation: to be praised by honest men, and to be abused by rogues. It is best, however, to secure the former, because it will invariably be accompanied by the latter.

Charles Caleb Colton, cleric (1780–1832), *Lacon: or Many Things in Few Words Addressed to those who Think* (1820)

You can't build a reputation on what you are going to do.

Henry Ford, industrialist (1863–1947)

In business a reputation for keeping absolutely to the letter and spirit of an agreement, even when it is unfavourable, is the most precious of assets, although it is not entered in the balance sheet.

Oliver Lyttelton, 1st Viscount Chandos (1893–1972), *Memoirs of Lord Chandos: An Unexpected View from the Summit* (1963)

❝ Responsibility

Responsibilities gravitate to the person who can shoulder them: power flows to the man who knows how.

Elbert Hubbard, philosopher (1856–1915), *The Philistine*

❝ Retirement

They say the number one killer of old people is retirement. People got 'em a job to do, they tend to live a little longer so they can do it.

Budd, character in *Kill Bill: Volume 2* (feature film, 2004)

There's never enough time to do all the nothing you want.

Calvin and Hobbes cartoon

66 Risk

Risk comes from not knowing what you're doing.

Warren Buffett, investor (1930–)

A man can well afford to be as bold as brass, my good fellow, when he gets gold in exchange!

Charles Dickens, novelist (1812–70), *Martin Chuzzlewit* (1843–44)

Anxiety [is] experiencing failure in advance ... if you have anxiety about initiating a project, then of course you will associate risk with failure.

Seth Godin, entrepreneur (1960–), *Poke the Box* (2011)

You'll always miss 100% of the shots you don't take.

Wayne Gretzky, ice-hockey player (1961–)

If you're not making mistakes, you're not taking risks, and that means you're not going anywhere. The key is to make mistakes faster than the competition, so you have more chances to learn and win.

John Holt, writer (1948–), *Fast Company*, October 1971

All courses of action are risky, so prudence is not in avoiding danger (it's impossible), but calculating risk and acting decisively. Make mistakes of ambition and not mistakes of sloth. Develop the strength to do bold things, not the strength to suffer.

Niccolò Machiavelli, philosopher (1469–1527), *The Prince* (1532)

Risk taking is inherently failure-prone. Otherwise, it would be called sure-thing-taking.

Tim McMahon, businessman

You can be living happily in the belly of a whale and operating with that as your world until one day the whale's belly contracts and you discover there is a whole universe of risks out there.

Paulo Rabello de Castro, economist, quoted in *The Economist*, May 2009

A ship in harbour is safe but that is not what ships are for.

John Shedd, academic (1859–unknown), *Salt From My Attic* (1928)

S

❝ The sack

He was fired with enthusiasm because he wasn't fired with enthusiasm.

Anon

Don't think of it as getting fired. Think of it as finally being recognised for your incompetence.

Cartoon in the *New Yorker*, October 2011

The things you get fired for when you're young are the same things you win lifetime achievement awards for when you're old.

Frances Ford Coppola (1939–), film director, interview with *Harvard Business Review*, September 2011

The PM is not going to sack you after a week. Sacked after 12 months, looks like you've fucked up. Sacked after a week, looks like he's fucked up.

Malcolm Tucker, character in *The Thick of It* (British TV series, 2005)

66 Science

The scientific industry has its exact counterpart in the kind of minds it harnesses: they no longer need to do themselves any violence in becoming their own voluntary and zealous overseers. Even if they show themselves, outside their official capacity, to be quite human and sensible beings, they are paralysed by pathic stupidity the moment they begin to think professionally.

Theodor Adorno, sociologist (1903–69)

66 Secretaries

And so while the great ones depart to their dinner,
the secretary stays, growing thinner and thinner,
racking his brain to record and report
what he thinks that they think that they ought to
    have thought.

Arthur Bryant, historian (1899–1985)

Always be nice to secretaries. They are the real gatekeepers in the world.

Anthony D'Angelo, education consultant, *The College Blue Book* (1995)

Behind every genius in business is an assistant telling him which buttons to press to get the telephone to work

Gene Perret, comedy writer

66 Self-employment

The unfortunate thing about working for yourself is
that you have the worst boss in the world. I work
every day of the year except at Christmas, when I
work a half day.

David Eddings, author (1931–2009)

Working for yourself sometimes ain't all that it's
    cracked up to be,
It can be as lonely at the top as at the bottom of that
    corporate tree.

Hoodoo Gurus, *1000 Miles Away*

Regard yourself as a small corporation of one. Take
yourself off on team-building exercises (long walks).
Hold a Christmas party every year at which you
stand in the corner of your writing room, shouting
very loudly to yourself while drinking a bottle of
white wine. Then masturbate under the desk. The
following day you will feel a deep and cohering
sense of embarrassment.

Will Self, writer (1961–), the *Guardian*, February 2010

66 Self-interest

Capital must be propelled by self-interest; it cannot
be enticed by benevolence.

Walter Bagehot, businessman, writer and early editor of *The
Economist* (1826–77), *Economic Studies* (1879)

Why should I disguise what you know so well, but what the crowd never dream of? We companies are all birds of prey; mere birds of prey. The only question is, whether in serving our own turn, we can serve yours too; whether in double-lining our own nest, we can put a single living into yours.

Charles Dickens, novelist (1812–70), *Martin Chuzzlewit* (1843–44)

Of course none of us is greedy – it's only the other fellow who is greedy. The world runs on individuals pursuing their self interests. The great achievements of civilisation have not come from government bureaus. Einstein didn't construct his theory under order from a bureaucrat. Henry Ford didn't revolutionise the automobile industry that way.

Milton Friedman, economist (1912–2006), talking on the *Phil Donohue Show*

❝ Selling

No sale is really complete until the product is worn out, and the customer is satisfied.

L.L. Bean, businessman (1872–1967)

Prospects don't care about you. They care about themselves, and anything they have to read or listen to that is not related to them is of little or no interest. Period. End of conversation. No questions asked.

Jay Conrad Levinson and **Al Lautenslager**, *Guerrilla Marketing in 30 Days* (2005)

A salesman has got to dream, boy. It comes with the territory.

Arthur Miller, playwright (1915–2005), *Death of a Salesman*

Everyone lives by selling something, whatever be his right to it. The burglar sells at the same time his own skill and courage and my silver plate ... The bandit sells the traveller an article of prime necessity: the traveller's life.

Robert Louis Stevenson, author (1850–94), *Across the Plains* (1892)

Awareness doesn't sell. All it does is get you in the consideration set. Then you sell.

Sergio Zymen, marketing executive (1945–), *The End of Marketing as We Know It* (1999)

66 Show business

If you're a car salesman, and someone says "This is a terrible car, I'm not buying it", it doesn't mean they hate you. They just don't like your product. I think that's a mistake a lot of people in show business make ... they're so tied to their act they take everything personally.

Jay Leno, chat-show host (1950–)

66 Small and medium-sized businesses

Don't dance where the elephants play.
German small business saying

66 Sport

It's just a job. Grass grows, birds fly, waves pound the sand. I beat people up.
Muhammad Ali, boxer (1942–)

We live by the Golden Rule. Those who have the gold make the rules.
Buzzie Bavasi, baseball manager (1914–2008)

Have you ever noticed what golf spells backwards?
Al Boliska, radio presenter (1942–72)

For a hundred years the owners screwed the players. For 25 years the players have screwed the owners – they've got 75 years to go.
Jim Bouton, baseball pitcher (1939–)

I call tennis the McDonald's of sport – you go in, they make a quick buck out of you, and you're out.
Pat Cash, tennis player (1965–)

If I had an argument with a player we would sit down for 20 minutes, talk about it and then decide I was right.

Brian Clough, football manager (1935–2004)

Rome wasn't built in a day. But I wasn't on that particular job.

Brian Clough

Business is a combination of war and sport.

André Maurois, author (1885–1967)

If I wanted to have an easy job I would have stayed at Porto. Beautiful blue chair, the UEFA Champions League trophy, God, and after God, me.

Jose Mourinho, football manager

The money coming into the game is incredible. But it is just the prune-juice effect – it comes in and goes out straight away. Agents run the game.

Alan Sugar, former football-club chairman (1947–)

66 Start-ups

The problem with the internet start-up craze isn't that too many people are starting companies; it's that too many people aren't sticking with it. That's somewhat understandable, because there are many moments that are filled with despair and agony, when you have to fire people and cancel things and deal with very difficult situations. That's when you find out who you are and what your values are. So when these people sell out, even though they get fabulously rich, they're gypping themselves out of one of the potentially most rewarding experiences of their unfolding lives. Without it, they may never know their values or how to keep their newfound wealth in perspective.

Steve Jobs, founder of Apple (1955–2011), quoted in *Fortune*, January 2000

Strategy

Speed, Price, Quality: Pick Two
Anon business adage

In civil business: what first? boldness; what second and third? boldness. And yet boldness is a child of ignorance and baseness, far inferior to other parts.
Francis Bacon, philosopher (1561–1626), *Of Boldness*

There are two ways to extend a business. Take inventory of what you're good at and extend out from your skills. Or determine what your customers need and work backward, even if it requires learning new skills.
Jeff Bezos, founder of Amazon (1964–)

There is something about the way that decisions get made in successful organisations that sows the seeds of eventual failure. Many large companies adopt a strategy of waiting until new markets are large enough to be interesting. But this is not often a successful strategy.

Clayton Christensen, academic (1952–), *The Innovator's Dilemma* (1997)

There are times at which it is right not to listen to customers, right to invest in developing lower-performance products that promise lower margins, and right to aggressively pursue small, rather than substantial, markets.

Clayton Christensen, *The Innovator's Dilemma* (1997)

One gets paid only for strengths; one does not get paid for weaknesses. The question, therefore, is first: What are our specific strengths? And then: Are they the right strengths? Are they the strengths that fit the opportunities of tomorrow, or are they the strengths that fitted those of yesterday? Are we deploying our strengths where the opportunities no longer are, or perhaps never were? And finally, what additional strengths do we have to acquire?

Peter Drucker, management writer (1909–2005), *Managing in Turbulent Times* (1980)

There is one rule for the industrialist and that is: make the best quality of goods possible at the lowest cost possible, paying the highest wages possible.

Henry Ford, industrialist (1863–1947)

If you can't pay for a thing, don't buy it. If you can't get paid for it, don't sell it. Do this, and you will have calm and drowsy nights, with all of the good business you have now and none of the bad. If you have time, don't wait for time.

Benjamin Franklin, polymath (1705–90)

You read a book from beginning to end. You run a business the opposite way. You start with the end, and then you do everything you must to reach it.

Harold Geneen, businessman (1910–97)

Strategy didn't start with Igor Ansoff, neither did it start with Machiavelli. It probably didn't start with Sun Tzu. Strategy is as old as human conflict.

Gary Hamel, management thinker (1954–)

An organisation becomes bewildered rather than energised when it's asked to do too much at once.

Michael Hammer and **James Champy**, *Reengineering the Corporation: A Manifesto for Business Revolution* (2004)

In a knowledge economy, a good business is a community with a purpose, not a piece of property.

Charles Handy, management thinker (1932–), *Harvard Business Review*, December 2002

Show competitors what you are doing. They will learn soon enough anyway. Just don't tell them what you are thinking.

Bill Hewlett, founder of Hewlett-Packard (1913–2001)

Sharing is to ownership what the iPod is to the eight-track, what the solar panel is to the coal mine. Sharing is clean, crisp, urbane, postmodern; owning is dull, selfish, timid, backward.

Mark Levine, poet (1965–), *New York Times*, March 2009

Sustained success is largely a matter of focusing regularly on the right things and making a lot of uncelebrated little improvements every day.

Theodore Levitt, academic (1925–2006), *Thinking in Management* (1983)

People don't want quarter-inch drills. They want quarter inch holes.

Theodore Levitt

Underpromise; overdeliver.

Tom Peters, management writer (1942–), quoted in the *Chicago Tribune*, June 1987

The essence of strategy is choosing what not to do.

Michael Porter, academic (1947–), *On Competition* (1998)

If you are shooting for second place, your strategy is determined by the leader.

Al Ries and **Jack Trout**, *The 22 Immutable Laws Of Marketing* (1994)

Bring out the three old warhorses of competition – cost, quality, and service – and drive them to new levels, making every person in the organisation see them for what they are, a matter of survival.

Jack Welch, businessman (1935–), *Winning: The Ultimate Business How-To Book* (2005)

If you don't have a competitive advantage, don't compete.

Jack Welch, *Six Rules of Successful Leadership*

❝ Success

However successful a man may be in his own business, if he turns from that and engages ill a business which he don't understand, he is like Samson when shorn of his locks his strength has departed, and he becomes like other men.

P.T. Barnum, showman (1810–91), *The Art of Money Getting* (1880)

Real success in business is to be found in achievements comparable rather with those of the artist or the scientist, of the inventor or statesman. And the joys sought in the profession of business must be like their joys and not the mere vulgar satisfaction which is experienced in the acquisition of money, in the exercise of power or in the frivolous pleasure of mere winning.

Louis Brandeis, lawyer (1856–1941), *La Follette's Weekly Magazine*, November 1912

Success is often achieved by those who don't know that failure is inevitable.

Coco Chanel, fashion designer (1883–1971)

The cool thing about Silicon Valley's brand of experimentation is that failure is often just slow success.

Cory Doctorow, writer (1971–), *Publishers Weekly*, June 2010

Try not to become a man of success but rather try to become a man of value.

Albert Einstein, scientist (1879–1955), *Einstein and the Poet* by William Hermanns (1983)

If A is success in life, then A = x + y + z. Work is x, play is y and z is keeping your mouth shut.

Albert Einstein

Don't aim for success – the more you aim at it and make it a target, the more you are going to miss it. For success, like happiness, cannot be pursued; it must ensue, and it only does so as the unintended side-effect of one's dedication to a cause greater than oneself or as the by-product of one's surrender to a person other than oneself. Happiness must happen, and the same holds for success: you have to let it happen by not caring about it.

Viktor Frankl, neurologist (1905–97), *In Search of Meaning* (1959)

It is those who are successful ... who are most likely
to be given the kinds of special opportunities that
lead to further success. It's the rich who get the
biggest tax breaks. It's the best students who get the
best teaching and most attention. And it's the biggest
nine- and ten-year-olds who get the most coaching
and practice. Success is the result of what sociologists
like to call "accumulative advantage".

Malcolm Gladwell, writer (1963–), *Outliers: The Story of Success* (1976)

My grandmother came to this country with $20 in
her pocket. She worked hard her whole life and
never took shit from anyone. When she died, she
had turned that $20 into $2,000. That sucks! You
know why she didn't succeed? Because she didn't
take shit from anyone. The key to success, and they
will not teach you in business school, is taking shit.

Nick Hendricks, character in *Horrible Bosses* (feature film, 2011)

Genius is often only the power of making
continuous efforts. The line between failure and
success is so fine that we scarcely know when we
pass it – so fine that we are often on the line and do
not know it. How many a man has thrown up his
hands at a time when a little more effort, a little
more patience, would have achieved success. As the
tide goes clear out, so it comes clear in. In business
sometimes prospects may seem darkest when really
they are on the turn. A little more persistence, a little

more effort, and what seemed hopeless failure may turn to glorious success. There is no failure except in no longer trying. There is no defeat except from within, no really insurmountable barrier save our own inherent weakness of purpose.

Elbert Hubbard, philosopher (1856–1915), *Electrical Review*, 1895

A man's success in business today turns upon his power of getting people to believe he has something that they want.

Gerald Stanley Lee, writer (1862–1944), *Crowds* (1914)

The difference between a successful person and others is not a lack of strength, not a lack of knowledge, but rather in a lack of will.

Vince Lombardi, American football coach (1913–70)

Success is like winning the sweepstakes or getting killed in an automobile crash. It always happens to somebody else.

Allan Sherman, writer (1924–73), *A Gift of Laughter* (1965)

Success is simply a matter of luck. Ask any failure.

Earl Wilson, writer (1907–87)

I couldn't wait for success, so I went ahead without it.

Jonathan Winters, comedian (1925–)

66 Supply chains

[The supply chain] stretches all the way from your supplier's suppliers to your customer's customers.

Anon (possibly coined by A.T. Kearney, management consultants)

Supply chains cannot tolerate even 24 hours of disruption. So if you lose your place in the supply chain because of wild behaviour you could lose a lot. It would be like pouring cement down one of your oil wells.

Thomas Friedman, writer (1953–), interview with Amazon. com

T

66 Talent

For almost a generation, psychologists around the world have been engaged in a spirited debate over a question that most of us would consider to have been settled years ago. The question is this: is there such a thing as innate talent? The obvious answer is yes. Not every hockey player born in January ends up playing at the professional level. Only some do – the innately talented ones. Achievement is talent plus preparation. The problem with this view is that the closer psychologists look at the careers of the gifted, the smaller the role innate talent seems to play and the bigger role preparation seems to play.

Malcolm Gladwell, writer (1963–), *Outliers: The Story of Success* (1976)

We are told that talent creates its own opportunities. But it sometimes seems that intense desire creates not only its own opportunities, but its own talents.

Eric Hoffer, philosopher (1902–83)

Degrees of ability vary, but the basic principle remains the same: the degree of a man's independence, initiative and personal love for his work determines his talent as a worker and his worth as a man.

Ayn Rand, author (1905–82), *The Fountainhead* (1943)

The ability to deal with people is as purchasable a commodity as sugar or coffee, and I will pay more for that ability than for any other under the sun.

John D. Rockefeller, industrialist (1839–1937), attributed

Talent hits a target no one else can hit; Genius hits a target no one else can see. With people with only modest ability, modesty is mere honesty; but with those who possess great talent, it is hypocrisy.

Arthur Schopenhauer, philosopher (1788–1860)

It's just not possible any longer to figure it out from the top, and have everyone else following the orders of the "grand strategist". The organisations that will truly excel in the future will be the organisations that discover how to tap people's commitment and capacity to learn at all levels in an organisation.

Peter Senge, scientist (1947–), *The Fifth Discipline: The Art and Practice of The Learning Organization* (1990)

Taxes

The art of taxation consists in so plucking the goose
as to get the most feathers with the least hissing.

Jean Baptist Colbert, French minister of finance (1619–83),
attributed

My advice for those that die; declare the pennies on
your eyes.

George Harrison, musician (1949–2001), *Taxman* (The
Beatles, 1966)

I like to pay taxes. With them I buy civilisation.

Oliver Wendell Holmes junior, judge (1841–1935)

Indoors or out, no one relaxes
In March, that month of wind and taxes,
The wind will presently disappear,
The taxes last us all the year.

Ogden Nash, poet (1902–71), *Versus*

If, from the more wretched parts of the old world,
we look at those which are in an advanced stage of
improvement, we still find the greedy hand of
government thrusting itself into every corner and
crevice of industry, and grasping the spoil of the
multitude. Invention is continually exercised, to
furnish new pretences for revenues and taxation. It
watches prosperity as its prey and permits none to
escape without tribute.

Thomas Paine, founding father of America (1737–1809),
Rights of Man (1791)

Taxes are paid in the sweat of every man who labours.
Franklin D. Roosevelt, American president (1882–1945),
speech, 1932

Taxes are the chief business of a conqueror of the
world.
George Bernard Shaw, playwright (1856–1950), *Caesar and
Cleopatra*

The expenses of government, having for their object
the interest of all, should be borne by everyone, and
the more a man enjoys the advantages of society, the
more he ought to hold himself honoured in
contributing to those expenses.
Anne Robert Jacques Turgot, economist (1727–81)

Income tax returns are the most imaginative fiction
being written today.
Herman Wouk, author (1915–)

❝ Teamwork

Remember that a lone amateur built the Ark. A large
group of professionals built the Titanic.
Dave Barry, author (1947–), *25 Things I Have Learned in 50
Years*

To succeed as a team is to hold all of the members
accountable for their expertise.
Mitchell Caplan, businessman (1957–)

The leaders who work most effectively, it seems to me, never say "I". And that's not because they have trained themselves not to say "I". They don't think "I". They think "we"; they think "team". They understand their job to be to make the team function. They accept responsibility and don't sidestep it, but "we" gets the credit.

Peter Drucker, management writer (1909–2005), *Managing the Nonprofit Organization* (1990)

Good leadership requires you to surround yourself with people of diverse perspectives who can disagree with you without fear of retaliation.

Doris Kearns Goodwin, writer (1943–)

Individual commitment to a group effort – that is what makes a team work, a company work, a society work, a civilization work.

Vince Lombardi, American football coach (1913–70)

A group becomes a team when each member is sure enough of himself and his contribution to praise the skills of the others.

Norman Shidle, writer

I use not only all the brains I have, but all I can borrow.

Woodrow Wilson, American president (1856–1924)

Most men are individuals no longer so far as their business, its activities, or its moralities are concerned. They are not units but fractions.

Woodrow Wilson, address to the American Bar Association, 1910

66 Technology

We are stuck with technology when what we really want is just stuff that works.

Douglas Adams, author (1952–2001)

On two occasions I have been asked, "Pray, Mr Babbage, if you put into the machine wrong figures, will the right answers come out?" I am not able rightly to apprehend the kind of confusion of ideas that could provoke such a question.

Charles Babbage, father of the computer (1791–1871)

The factory of the future will have only two employees, a man and a dog. The man will be there to feed the dog. The dog will be there to keep the man from touching the equipment.

Warren Bennis, academic (1925–)

When a machine begins to run without human aid, it is time to scrap it – whether it be a factory or a government.

Alexander Chase, writer (1926–), *Perspectives* (1966)

In a world of abundant knowledge, hoarding technology is a self-limiting strategy. Nor can any organisation, even the largest, afford any longer to ignore the tremendous external pools of knowledge that exist.

Henry Chesborough, academic, *Open Innovation: The New Imperative for Creating and Profiting from Technology* (2003)

By and large, a disruptive technology is initially embraced by the least profitable customers in a market. Hence, most companies with a practiced discipline of listening to their best customers and identifying new products that promise greater profitability and growth are rarely able to build a case for investing in disruptive technologies until it is too late.

Clayton Christensen, academic (1952–), *The Innovator's Dilemma* (1997)

The most important and urgent problems of the technology of today are no longer the satisfactions of the primary needs or of archetypal wishes, but the reparation of the evils and damages by the technology of yesterday.

Dennis Gabor, electrical engineer (1900–79), *Innovations: Scientific, Technological and Social* (1970)

The first rule of any technology used in a business is that automation applied to an efficient operation will magnify the efficiency. The second is that automation applied to an inefficient operation will magnify the inefficiency.

Bill Gates, founder of Microsoft (1955–)

If GM had kept up with technology like the computer industry has, we would all be driving $25 cars that got 1000 MPG.

Bill Gates

One machine can do the work of 50 ordinary men. No machine can do the work of one extraordinary man.

Elbert Hubbard, philosopher (1856–1915), *A Message to Garcia* (1899)

The desktop computer industry is dead. Innovation has virtually ceased. Microsoft dominates with very little innovation. That's over. Apple lost. The desktop market has entered the dark ages, and it's going to be in the dark ages for the next ten years, or certainly for the rest of this decade. It's like when IBM drove a lot of innovation out of the computer industry before the microprocessor came along. Eventually, Microsoft will crumble because of complacency, and maybe some new things will grow. But until that happens, until there's some fundamental technology shift, it's just over.

Steve Jobs, founder of Apple (1955–2011), Quoted in *Wired* magazine, October 1996

For a list of all the ways technology has failed to improve the quality of life, please press three.
Alice Kahn, writer (1943–)

Western society has accepted as unquestionable a technological imperative that is quite as arbitrary as the most primitive taboo: not merely the duty to foster invention and constantly to create technological novelties, but equally the duty to surrender to these novelties unconditionally, just because they are offered, without respect to their human consequences.
Lewis Mumford, historian (1895–1990)

The Christian notion of the possibility of redemption is incomprehensible to the computer.
Vance Packard, writer (1914–96)

The chief product of an automated society is a widespread and deepening sense of boredom.
Cyril Northcote Parkinson, historian (1909–93)

If it weren't for the people, the god-damn people always getting tangled up in the machinery. If it weren't for them, the world would be an engineer's paradise.
Kurt Vonnegut, author (1992–2007), *Player Piano* (1952)

The IBM machine has no ethic of its own; what it does is enable one or two people to do the computing work that formerly required many more people. If people often use it stupidly, it's their stupidity, not the machine's, and a return to the abacus would not exorcise the failing. People can be treated as drudges just as effectively without modern machines.

William Whyte, writer (1917–99), *The Organization Man* (1956)

Civilisation requires slaves. The Greeks were quite right there. Unless there are slaves to do the ugly, horrible, uninteresting work, culture and contemplation become almost impossible. Human slavery is wrong, insecure and demoralising. On mechanical slavery, on the slavery of the machine, the future of the world depends.

Oscar Wilde, writer (1854–1900), *The Soul of Man Under Socialism* (1891)

❝ The tobacco industry

It is more profitable for your congressman to support the tobacco industry than your life.

Jackie Mason, comedian (1936–)

❝ Training

The only thing worse than training people and having them leave is not training them and having them stay

Zig Ziglar, writer (1926–)

U

❝ Unemployment

A man willing to work, and unable to find work, is perhaps the saddest sight that fortune's inequality exhibits under this sun.

Thomas Carlyle, historian (1795–1881), *Chartism* (1839)

An unemployed existence is a worse negation of life than death itself.

José Ortega y Gasset, philosopher (1883–1955), *The Revolt of the Masses* (1930)

What the country needs are a few labour-making inventions.

Arnold H. Glasow, humorist (1905–98)

The production of too many useful things results in too many useless people.

Karl Marx, philosopher (1818–83), *Economic and Philosophical Manuscripts* (1844)

Unemployment insurance is a pre-paid vacation for freeloaders.

Ronald Reagan, American president (1911–2004)

I grew up in the '30s with an unemployed father. He didn't riot. He got on his bike and looked for work, and he kept looking 'til he found it.

Norman Tebbit, politician (1931–), in response to the British riots of 1981

The trouble with unemployment is that the minute you wake up in the morning you're on the job.

Slappy White, comedian (1921–95)

Unions and industrial relations

Labour unions would have us believe that they transfer income from rich capitalists to poor workers. In fact, they mostly transfer income from the large number of non-union workers to a small number of relatively well-off union workers.

Robert Anderson, writer, *Just Get Out of the Way: How Government Can Help Business in Poor Countries* (2004)

Strong, responsible unions are essential to industrial fair play. Without them the labour bargain is wholly one-sided. The parties to the labour contract must be nearly equal in strength if justice is to be worked out, and this means that the workers must be organised and that their organisations must be recognised by employers as a condition precedent to industrial peace.

Louis Brandeis, lawyer (1856–1941), *The curse of bigness: Miscellaneous papers of Louis D. Brandeis* (1934)

With all their faults, trade-unions have done more for humanity than any other organisation of men that ever existed. They have done more for decency, for honesty, for education, for the betterment of the race, for the developing of character in man, than any other association of men.

Clarence Darrow, lawyer (1857–1938), *The Railroad Trainman* (1906)

The strike is the weapon of the oppressed, of men capable of appreciating justice and having the courage to resist wrong and contend for principle.

Eugene Debs, founder of the American Railroad Union (1855–1926)

All classes of society are trades unionists at heart, and differ chiefly in the boldness, ability, and secrecy with which they pursue their respective interests.

William Stanley Jevons, economist (1835–82), *The State in Relation to Labour* (1882)

No king on earth is as safe in his job as a Trade Union official. There is only one thing that can get him sacked; and that is drink. Not even that, as long as he doesn't actually fall down.

George Bernard Shaw, playwright (1856–1950), *The Apple Cart*

If you don't like your job you don't strike. You just go in every day and do it really half-assed. That's the American way.

Homer Simpson, character in *The Simpsons* (American TV series)

To remember the loneliness, the fear and the insecurity of men who once had to walk alone in huge factories, beside huge machines – to realise that labour unions have meant new dignity and pride to millions of our countrymen – human companionship on the job, and music in the home – to be able to see what larger pay cheques mean, not to a man as an employee, but as a husband and as a father – to know these things is to understand what American labour means.

Adlai Stevenson, politician (1900–65), *The Speeches of Adlai Stevenson* (1952)

The two sides of industry have traditionally always regarded each other in Britain with the greatest possible loathing, mistrust and contempt. They are both absolutely right.

Auberon Waugh, writer (1939–2001), *Private Eye*, December 1983

V

❝ Value

I saw an advertisement the other day for the secret of life. It said "The secret of life can be yours for 25 shillings. Send to Secret of Life Institute, Willesden." So I wrote away, seemed a good bargain, secret of life, 25 shillings. And I got a letter back saying, "If you think you can get the secret of life for 25 shillings, you don't deserve to have it. Send 50 shillings for the secret of life."

Peter Cook, satirist (1937–95), E.L. Wisty, "Are you spotty?"

Price is what you pay. Value is what you get.

Ben Graham, investor (1894–1976)

People want economy and they'll pay almost any price to get it.

Lee Iacocca, businessman (1924–)

Anything you lose automatically doubles in value.

Mignon McLaughlin, writer (1913–83), *The Second Neurotic's Notebook* (1966)

There is scarcely anything in the world that some man cannot make a little worse, and sell a little more cheaply. The person who buys on price alone is this man's lawful prey.

John Ruskin, critic (1819–1900)

W

❝ Wealth

Believe not much them that seem to despise riches,
for they despise them that despair of them.
Francis Bacon, philosopher (1561–1626), *Of Riches*

If I was as rich as Rockefeller I'd be richer than
Rockefeller, because I'd do a bit of window cleaning
on the side.
Ronnie Barker, comedian (1929–2005)

Whoever loves money never has money enough;
whoever loves wealth is never satisfied with his
income.
The Bible, Ecclesiastes 5:10

I don't pay good wages because I have a lot of
money; I have a lot of money because I pay good
wages.
Robert Bosch, industrialist (1861–1942)

I don't have a problem with guilt about money. The
way I see it is that my money represents an
enormous number of claim cheques on society. It is

like I have these little pieces of paper that I can turn into consumption. If I wanted to, I could hire 10,000 people to do nothing but paint my picture every day for the rest of my life. And the GNP would go up. But the utility of the product would be zilch, and I would be keeping those 10,000 people from doing AIDS research, or teaching, or nursing. I don't do that though. I don't use very many of those claim cheques. There's nothing material I want very much. And I'm going to give virtually all of those claim cheques to charity when my wife and I die.

Warren Buffett, investor (1930–)

The superfluities of a rich nation furnish a better object of trade than the necessities of a poor one. It is the interest of the commercial world that wealth should be found everywhere.

Edmund Burke, philosopher (1729–97), *Two Letters to Gentlemen of Bristol* (1778)

Fortune does not change men, it unmasks them.

Suzanne Curchod (aka Madame Necker), writer (1737–94)

The richest 1% of this country owns half our country's wealth, $5 trillion. One-third of that comes from hard work, two-thirds comes from inheritance, interest on interest accumulating to widows and idiot sons and what I do, stock and real estate speculation. It's bullshit. You got 90% of the American public out there with little or no net worth. I create nothing. I own. We make the rules, pal. The news, war, peace,

famine, upheaval, the price per paper clip. We pick
that rabbit out of the hat while everybody sits out
there wondering how the hell we did it. Now you're
not naive enough to think we're living in a
democracy, are you buddy? It's the free market.

Gordon Gekko, character in *Wall Street* (feature film, 1987)

If all the money and property in the world were
divided up equally at, say, three o'clock in the
afternoon, by 3.30 p.m. there would already be
notable differences in the financial conditions of the
recipients. Within that first thirty minutes, some
adults would have lost their share. Some would have
gambled theirs away, and some would have been
swindled out of their portion ... After ninety days, the
difference would be staggering. And, I'm willing to
wager that, within a year or two at the most, the
distribution of wealth would conform to patterns
almost identical with those that had previously
prevailed.

Jean Paul Getty, oil magnate (1892–1976), *As I See It* (1976)

Riches may not make you any friends, but they
greatly increase the class and variety of your
enemies.

Audric Goldfinger, villain in *Goldfinger* by Ian Fleming (1959)

There is a burden of care in getting riches, fear in
keeping them, temptation in using them, sorrow in

losing them, and a burden of account at last to be given up concerning them.

Matthew Henry, Presbyterian minister (1662–1714), *Dictionary of Burning Words of Brilliant Writers* (1895)

Get rich, if you will – you take great risks. But Christianity does not say to any man, "You must be worth only so much, extend your business only so far." It says, "Use your riches for the glory of God." If they once usurp His place, woe to you!

Herrick Johnson, Presbyterian minister (1832–1913), *Dictionary of Burning Words of Brilliant Writers* (1895)

If I hadn't been very rich, I might have been a really great man.

Charles Foster Kane, character in *Citizen Kane* (feature film, 1941)

People who are rich want to be richer, but what's the difference? The toys get different, that's all. The rich guys buy a football team, the poor guys buy a football. It's all relative.

Martina Navratilova, tennis player (1956–), *Martina* (1987)

You can't tell a millionaire's son from a billionaire's.

Vance Packard, writer (1914–96), *The Status Seekers* (1959)

Don't knock the rich. When did a poor person give you a job?

Laurence Peter, teacher and writer (1919–90)

With $10,000, we'd be millionaires! We could buy all kinds of useful things like ... love!

Homer Simpson, character in *The Simpsons* (American TV series)

Of course, there's a different law for the rich and the poor: otherwise, who would go into business?

E. Ralph Stewart

Nothing is more admirable than the fortitude with which millionaires tolerate the disadvantages of their wealth.

Rex Stout, author (1886–1975), *The Red Box* (1937)

66 Women in business

I don't play golf. I don't go to the men's room. I didn't have the ability to network the way men do.

Jill Barad, businesswomen (1951–)

A number of studies have shown that women who promote their own interests vigorously are seen as aggressive, uncooperative, and selfish. An equal number of studies show that the failure of women to promote their own interests results in a lack of female leaders.

Joanna Barsh, **Susie Cranston** and **Rebecca A. Craske**, "Centered leadership: How talented women thrive", *McKinsey Quarterly*, September 2008

The point at which some woman starts up a business and nobody cares about it, that's when we'll all know we made it.

Barbara Cassani, businesswoman (1960–)

People assume you slept your way to the top. Frankly, I couldn't sleep my way to the middle.

Joni Evans, businesswoman (1942–)

Women do not win formula one races, because they simply are not strong enough to resist the G-forces. In the boardroom, it is different. I believe women are better able to marshal their thoughts than men and because they are less egotistical they make fewer assumptions.

Nicola Foulsten, former motor racing manager (1972–), quoted in the *Independent*, April 1995

Many women say, "I have enough money." I rarely hear a man say that.

Myra Hart, academic (1940–), "How Women Can Get More Venture Capital", interview with *HBS Working Knowledge* (2004)

It's so much easier for men. They don't have to paint their nails for a meeting.

Eve Pollard, journalist (1945–), quoted in the *Guardian*, December 1995

Women are just men with less money.

Paul Samuelson, economist (1915–2009)

I have yet to hear a man ask for advice on how to combine marriage and a career.

Gloria Steinem, writer (1934–)

Men are taught to apologise for their weaknesses, women for their strengths.

Lois Wyse, advertising executive (1926–2007)

❝ Work-life balance

There is time for work, and time for love. That leaves no other time.

Coco Chanel, fashion designer (1883–1971)

How many people on their deathbed wish they'd spent more time at the office?

Stephen Covey, author (1932–), *First Things First* (1994)

Total commitment to family and total commitment to career is possible, but fatiguing.

Muriel Fox, businesswoman, quoted in *New Woman*, October 1972

No one will be buried with the epitaph "he maximised shareholder value".

John Kay, economist (1948–), *Obliquity: Why Our Goals Are Best Achieved Indirectly* (2011)

No man tastes pleasures truly, who does not earn
them by previous business; and few people do
business well, who do nothing else.
Philip Dormer Stanhope, 4th Earl of Chesterfield (1694–
1773), letter to his son

Perpetual devotion to what a man calls his business,
is only to be sustained by perpetual neglect of many
other things.
Robert Louis Stevenson, author (1850–94), *Virginibus
Puerisque* (1881)

For fast-acting relief, try slowing down.
Lily Tomlin, actor (1939–)

Every time you think about your work-life balance
issue, remember what your boss is thinking about
– and that's winning. Your needs may get heard
– and even successfully resolved – but not if the
boss's needs aren't met as well.
Jack Welch, businessman (1935–), *Winning: The Ultimate
Business How-To Book* (2005)

Work-life moaners tend to be a phenomenon of
below-average performers.
Jack Welch, *Winning: The Ultimate Business How-To Book*
(2005)

Acknowledgements

I would like to thank Daniel Crewe, Lisa Owens,
Penny Williams and Stephen Brough at Profile Books
for their support. Thanks also to the work-experience
students who helped me scour back issues of *The
Economist*, including Abdul Qabir Jaha, Megan Cully,
Rhiannon Rees and Dimple Vijaykumar. Lastly, this
book would not have been possible without the
patience of Lyndsey, who turned a blind eye to my
sneaking a laptop on several family holidays, or the
consideration of Iris, who didn't show up too soon.

Bill Ridgers
April 2012

Index

Fictional names are indexed in quotation marks under the surname.

Achor, Shawn 104
Ackoff, Russell 142
Adair, John 33
Adams, Douglas 74, 176, 210
Adams, Henry 152
Addison, Joseph 169
Ade, George 26
Adolt, H.V. 176
Adorno, Theodor 15, 67, 68, 104, 190
Aeschylus 81, 131
Aiken, Howard 112
Albee, Edward 124
Ali, Muhammad 194
Allchin, Jim 95
Amabile, Teresa 104
Ambler, Eric 82
Anardoko Petroleum Corporation 166
Anderson, Robert 216
Anglo Persian Oil Company 175
Anon 1, 20, 27, 33, 45, 56, 109, 112, 133, 140, 189, 196, 204

Aristotle 109
Aston, Elizabeth 15
Auden, W.H. 127
Austen, Jane 140

Babbage, Charles 210
Bacon, Francis 135, 196, 221
Bagehot, Walter 43, 54, 191
"Bagley, Denis Dimbleby" 3
Bahá'u'lláh 109
Bailey, Archbishop LeRoy, junior 82
Ballard, J.G. 46
Balzac, Honoré de 68, 101, 130
Bamford, Joseph 70
Barad, Jill 225
Barker, Ronnie 37, 221
Barnes, Michael 44
Barnum, P.T. 3, 36, 58, 156, 200
Barratt, Matthew 95
Barry, Dave 26, 208
Barsh, Joanna 225
Bartz, Carol 86
Baudelaire, Charles 109
Baudrillard, Jean 163

Bavasi, Buzzie 194
Bayan, Rick 49
Bean, L.L. 192
Beaton, Cecil 118
Beaverbrook, Lord 97,
   105
Beckett, Samuel 89
Beene, Geoffrey 15
Benchley, Robert 38
Bennett, Arnold 85
Bennis, Warren 61,
   135–36, 143, 210
Bergen, Edgar 10, 37, 105
Bernanke, Ben 93
Bernstein, Paula 49
Bezos, Jeff 49, 112, 118,
   175, 196
Bible, The
   Ecclesiastes 221
   Matthew 156
   Proverbs 9, 102, 105,
      105
   St Luke 131
Bierce, Ambrose 49, 63,
   99, 185
"Bilko, Sergeant Ernest"
   91, 183
Billings, Josh 157
Biver, Jean-Claude 56
"Blackadder, Edmund"
   20
Blankfein, Lloyd 16
Bohr, Niels 87, 172
Bok, Derek 76
Boliska, Al 112, 194
Bombeck, Erma 32

Bonfield, Peter 155
Booth, Charles 168
Booth, William 127,
   171–72
Bosch, Robert 221
Boswell, Nelson 56
Boulding, Kenneth 72,
   80, 103
Bouton, Jim 194
Bovee, Christian Nestell
   44, 106, 136
Brandeis, Louis 82, 109,
   200, 216
Branson, Richard 144
Braschi, Giannina 16
Brewster, Kingman,
   junior 153
Brin, Sergey 113
Britt, Stuart Henderson 3
Bronfman, Edward,
   senior 120
Brooks, Arthur 77–78
Browning, Guy 14, 38,
   43, 45, 140–41, 164–65,
   180–81
Bryant, Arthur 190
Buckingham, Marcus 144
"Budd" (in Kill Bill:
   Volume 2) 186
Buffett, Warren 1, 55, 94,
   101, 111, 118, 120, 121,
   151, 155, 185, 187,
   221–22
Burchill, Julie 168–69
Burke, Edmund 222
Burnett, Leo 4, 97

Burnett, T-Bone 159–60
"Burns, Monty" 96
Burr, Donald 82
Burton, Robert 11
Bushnell, Nolan 157
Buxbaum, Martin 6
Buzzell, Robert 26
Byron, Lord 21

Calvin and Hobbes
   cartoon 187
Campbell, Bill 49
Camus, Albert 157
Canterbury, Tim 165
Caplan, Mitchell 208
Capone, Al 29, 55
Carey, Drew 37, 165
Carey, Phillip 47
Carlyle, Thomas 128, 153,
   183, 215
Carnegie, Andrew 41, 50,
   66, 106
Carnegie, Dale 148
Carpenters' mantra 172
Cash, Pat 194
Cassani, Barbara 226
Cerf, Vinton 118
Champy, James 198
Chandler, Raymond 83
Chanel, Coco 201, 229
Chase, Alexander 210
Chesborough, Henry 211
Chesterton, G.K. 38, 74
Chomsky, Noam 47
Christensen, Clayton 113,
   196–97, 211

Chrysler, Walter 133
Churchill, Winston 29,
   39, 178
Cicero, Marcus Tullius 54
Citizen Kane (film) 85, 91
Cleese, John 1, 15, 16–17
Clough, Brian 195
Coase, Ronald 61
Coffin, Harold 56
Coffman, Curt 144
Coggan, Philip 155
Coke, Edward 131
Colbert, Jean Baptist 207
Collins, Jim 24
Colony, George 56
Colton, Charles Caleb
   81, 185–86
Confucius 104
Cook, Peter 4, 113, 173,
   219
Cooley, Mason 166
Coolidge, Calvin 12, 178
Coppola, Frances Ford
   189
"Corleone, Michael" 96
Coupland, Douglas 154
Covey, Stephen 229
Cowell, Simon 12
Cox, Harvey 64
Cranston, Susie 225
Craske, Rebecca A. 225
Cuban, Mark 89
Curchod, Suzanne (aka
   Madame Necker) 222

Dahlberg, Edward 61

D'Angelo, Anthony 190
Daniel, Vincent 93
Darin, Bobby 160
Darrow, Clarence 217
De Bono, Edward 142
De Castro, Paulo Rabello
      188
DeBry, David 99–100
Debs, Eugene 217
Deming, W. Edwards 61,
      87
Deng Xiaoping 32
DeWolf, Nicholas 57
Dickens, Charles 21,
      33–34, 63–64, 68, 130,
      162, 187, 192
Dickey, Parke 166
Dilbert comic strip 51, 86,
      87–88, 114, 165–66
Dillard, Annie 51
Doctorow, Cory 201
Dodge, W.E. 179
Doriot, George 176
"Draper, Donald" 4, 91
Drucker, Peter 51, 55, 57,
      64, 72, 114, 125, 143,
      144, 149, 177, 197, 209
Dumas, Alexandre 54
Durant, Will 17
Dylan, Bob 44, 157

Economist, The 94, 99
Eddings, David 191
Eddison, Alan 80
Edison, Thomas 89, 106,
      107, 167, 179

Edwards, Sherman 131
Ehrenreich, Barbara
      70–71
Einstein, Albert 104, 201
Eisenhower, Dwight D.
      175
Emerson, Ralph Waldo
      138, 144
Eno, Brian 125
Erickson, Arthur 92
Evans, Joni 226

"Fawlty, Basil" 57
Feldman, Mark 64
Feynman, Richard 72
Fforde, Jasper 101
Field, Marshall 41
Firestone, Harvey 64
Fisher, Irving 175
Fitzgerald, F. Scott 43
Forbes, Malcolm 108
Ford, Henry 57, 83, 86,
      89, 159, 163, 177, 186,
      197
Fortune cookie motto 90
Foulsten, Nicola 226
Fox, Muriel 229
France, Anatole 54
Frankl, Victor 201
Franklin, Benjamin 103,
      136, 198
Frecht, Utz 21
Frenckner, Paulsson
      144–45
Friedman, Milton 24, 93,
      152, 192

Friedman, Thomas 29, 39–40, 44, 77, 80, 167, 170, 204

Gabor, Dennis 211
Gaherin, John 157
Galbraith, John Kenneth 17
Gandhi, Mahatma 58, 102
Gates, Bill 58, 76, 212
"Gekko, Gordon" 91, 94, 96, 102, 157, 222–23
Geneen, Harold 7, 61, 77, 133, 171, 198
George, Susan 81, 155
Gerber, Michael 78
German small business saying 194
Getty, Jean Paul 167, 223
Gladwell, Malcolm 51, 65, 78–79, 107, 124, 202, 205
Glasow, Arnold H. 46, 179, 215
Gobel, George 70
Godin, Seth 34, 51–52, 58, 90, 105, 149, 187
Goffee, Rob 56
"Goldfinger, Audric" 223
Goldsmith, Marshall 11
Goldsmith, Oliver 83
Goldwyn, Sam 131
Goleman, Daniel 61–62
Goodwin, Doris Kearns 209

Google 84
Gotti, John 22
Graham, Ben 219
Green, Harold 87
Gretzky, Wayne 187
Grove, Andrew 34

Half, Robert 66
Hamel, Gary 34, 41, 125–26, 136, 145, 156, 198
Hamilton, Alexander 180, 184
Hamilton, William Peter 114
Hammer, Michael 198
Handy, Charles 79, 198
Hanlon, Robert J. 7
Hannum, David 58
Haque, Umair 12–13
Hargadon, Andrew 114
Harrison, George 207
Hart, Myra 226
Havel, Vaclav 84
Hayek, Friedrich 73
Hazlitt, William 124
Heatter, Gabriel 22
Heidegger, Martin 9
Heller, Joseph 45
Helps, Arthur 109–10
Hendricks, Nick 202
Henry, Matthew 223–24
Herring, Richard 37, 133
Hesburgh, Theodore 136
Hewlett, Bill 198
Hicks, Bill 55

Hilton, Anthony 17
Hock, Dee 25
Hoff, Benjamin 47
Hoffer, Eric 29, 115, 164, 205
Holland, Xaviera 169
Hollis, Nigel 23
Holmes, Oliver Wendell, junior 207
Holt, John 187
Hoodoo Gurus 191
Hopper, Grace 115
Hsi Tang Chih Tsang 102
Hubbard, Elbert 79, 90, 107, 115, 133–34, 186, 202–3, 212
Huffman, Brigadier General Gary E. 7
Hugo, Victor 169, 180
Hunt, Tara 177

Iacocca, Lee 176, 219
IBM 175
Iyengar, Sheena 150

Jackson, Jesse 134
Jay-Z 161
Jefferson, Thomas 4, 17–18, 19
Jerome, Jerome K. 130, 134
Jevons, William Stanley 217
Jobs, Steve 7, 66–67, 97, 115, 119, 195–96, 212
Johnson, Herrick 224

Johnson, Samuel 128, 173
Joke 2, 184
Jones, John Harvey 172–73

Kafka, Franz 132
Kahn, Alice 213
Kahneman, Daniel 138, 170
Kamprad, Ingvar 7
"Kane, Charles Foster" 224
Kanter, Rosabeth Moss 174
Kaplan, Robert 62
Kassaei, Amir 23
Kay, Alan 90, 116
Kay, John 229
Kellaway, Lucy 142
Kelleher, Herb 9, 22, 103
Kellems, Vivien 98
Keller, Maryann 32
Kennedy, Mark 134
Kennedy, Paul 35
Keynes, John Maynard 13, 19, 30, 73, 121, 152, 158, 182
Khrushchev, Nikita 58
Khurana, Rakesh 13
Kim, W. Chan 41
King, Stephen 23–24
Kipling, Rudyard 90
Kissinger, Henry 28
Klein, Naomi 30, 100
Knusden, William 41
Kocher, Gerhard 71

Kotler, Philip 24, 143, 150, 152
Kotter, John 39
Kroc, Ray 50
Krugman, Paul 93
Kundera, Milan 150
Kutagari, Ken 111

Laertius, Diogenes 69
Lagerfeld, Karl 32
Laker, Freddie 42
Latimer, A.A. 2
Lautenslager, Al 192
Leacock, Stephen 5
Lee, Brenda 160
Lee, Gerald Stanley 203
Lee Kun-Hee 35
Lee Myung-Bak 71
Lenin, Vladimir 2
Lennox, Annie 160
Leno, Jay 193
Letterman, David 2
Levine, Mark 199
Levinson, Jay Conrad 192
Levitt, Theodore 100, 143, 199
Lewis, Michael 19, 94, 122
Lilly, Doris 166
Lincoln, Abraham 173
Lippman, Greg 184
Lippman, Walter 107
Little, Royal 179
Livingstone, David 100
Lombardi, Vince 97, 107, 137, 203, 209

Lü Buwei 83
Lundborg, Louis 84
Lynch, Peter 122
Lynn, Loretta 160
Lyttelton, Oliver, 1st Viscount Chandos 186

McCarthy, Mary 86
McClane, John 180
McCormack, Mark 7
McGovan, William 103
McGovern, William 108
McGregor, Douglas 145
McGuire, Barry 161
Machiavelli, Niccolò 187–88
McLaughlin, Mignon 219
McLuhan, Marshall 5, 116
McMahon, Tim 188
Malcolm X (Malcolm Little) 154
March, James 116
Marcus, H. Stanley 59
Marx, Karl 30–31, 40, 215
Mason, Jackie 214
Máté, Ferenc 48
Mauborgne, Renée 42
Maugham, W. Somerset 92
Maurois, André 195
Maynard, Micheline 32–33
Mayo, William James 124
Mead, Margaret 141

Meir, Golda 167, 178
Mencken, H.L. 158
Microsoft 77
Miller, Arthur 193
Miller, Bryan 27
Miller, Dennis 37, 97
Miller, Henry 137
Mills, C. Wright 92
Mintzberg, Henry 26–27,
    137, 145–46
Montapert, Alfred 96,
    180
Morgan, John Pierpont
    132, 159, 164, 176
Morita, Akio 100, 116
Morrison, Van 161
Morrissey 161
Mortimer, John 11
Mourinho, Jose 195
Mumford, Lewis 213

Nader, Ralph 118, 167
Napoleon Bonaparte 7
Nash, Ogden 19, 207
Nasreddin, Mulla 87
Navratilova, Martina 224
Nevill, Dorothy 39
New Yorker 189
Newton, Isaac 122
Nicholson, Jack 93
Nielsen, Leslie 134
Noebel, David 125
Nohria, Nitin 13
Nordstrom, Kjell 22
Norton, David 62
Nunez, Oscar 137

Ogilvy, David 6, 48, 108,
    147, 150–51, 154, 156
Ohmae, Kenichi 101
O'Leary, Michael 10, 81
Oliver, Vic 158
Onassis, Aristotle 7–8
Orben, Robert 110
O'Rourke, P.J. 40
Ortega y Gasset, José
    215
Orwell, George 6, 130
Owen, Robert 110

Packard, Vance 52, 213,
    224
Paine, Thomas 207
Palahniuk, Chuck 48
Parker, Dorothy 74, 184
Parker, Peter 79
Parkinson, Cyril
    Northcote 65, 177, 213
Pascale, Richard 35, 117
Patton, George 177
Peale, Norman Vincent
    11
Penrice, Daniel 13
Pepper, Claude 173
Peppers, Don 59
Perot, Ross 33, 38
Perret, Gene 190
Peter, Laurence 25, 132,
    181, 224
Peters, Tom 8, 85, 119, 137,
    143, 199
Petronis, Gale 92
"Picard, Jean-Luc" 164

Plain English Campaign
141

Poincaré, Henri 117

Pollard, Eve 226

Pope, Alexander 172

Porter, Michael 199

Pournelle, Jerry 27

Prahalad, C.K. 79, 136,
143, 156, 173–74

Pratt, Wallace 167

Preis, Michael 146

Presley, Elvis 2, 11

Proverb 85

Rand, Ayn 14, 52–53, 69,
110, 158, 205–6

Ratner, Gerald 95

Reagan, Ronald 125,
215

Revson, Charles 6

Ridderstrale, Jonas
22

Ries, Al 24, 35, 42, 117,
151, 152, 199

Robertson, Dennis
Holme 174

Robin, Vicki 14

Rockefeller, John D. 45,
85, 96, 159, 206

Rockefeller, John D.,
junior 103

Roddick, Anita 79–80,
148

Rogers, Martha 59

Roosevelt, Franklin D.
208

Roosevelt, Theodore 23,
81, 146, 178

Rothbard, Murray 102

"Rothstein, Sam 'Ace'"
99

Rousseau, Jean-Jacques
122

Roy, Arundhati 67–68

Rumelt, Richard 62

Ruskin, John 147, 184, 220

Samuelson, Paul 73, 86,
123, 226

Sarnoff, David 42

Saul, John Ralston 19

Schmidt, Eric 84

Schopenhauer, Arthur
206

Schultz, Peter 109

Schumpeter, Joseph 31,
70

Scott, Howard 55

Scott, Michael 146

Sculley, John 62

Seidenberg, Ivan 95

Self, Will 191

Seneca 138

Senge, Peter 35–36, 60,
87, 156, 206

Shakespeare, William
132, 162

Shapiro, Benson 42

Shapiro, Stephen 117

Shaw, George Bernard
20, 36, 39, 73, 105, 164,
180, 208, 217

Shedd, John 188
Shenkir, William 185
Shepard, Sam 151
Shepherd, David 96
Shepherd, Freddie 96
Sherman, Allan 203
Shidle, Norman 209
Short, Clare 101
Shugrue, Martin 10
Silvestrini, Cardinal
    Achille 85
Simon, Herbert 62, 63
"Simpson, Homer" 8, 63,
    218, 225
Sloan, Alfred 63, 65, 181
Slywotzky, Adrian
    40-41
Smiles, Samuel 31, 107,
    110
Smith, Adam 74-75,
    128-29, 182, 183
"Sollozzo" 55, 91
Sowell, Thomas 3, 31, 75,
    88, 108, 155, 176, 185
Spratt, Michael 64
Stanhope, Philip
    Dormer, 4th Earl of
    Chesterfield 228
Staubach, Roger 59
Stein, Herbert 48, 59
Steinbeck, John 53,
    69
Steinem, Gloria 229
Stelzer, Irwin 156
Stemp, Josiah 20
Stevenson, Adlai 218

Stevenson, Robert Louis
    193, 228
Stew Leonard's 59
Stewart, E. Ralph 225
Stewart, Thomas 50
Stout, Rex 225
Stowell, William 28
Sugar, Alan 195
Surowiecki, James 69
Sutton, Robert 23
Swaffer, Helen 153

Taleb, Nassim Nicholas
    27, 46, 50, 70, 138-39
Tammeus, William 168
Taylor, Frederick
    Winslow 129, 134
Tebbit, Norman 216
Tedlow, Richard 40-41
Templar, Richard 59
Thalberg, Irving 40
Thatcher, Margaret 40,
    108, 141, 159, 178
Thompson, Hunter S.
    132, 153
Thomson, Adam 10
Thoreau, Henry David
    12, 129, 131, 180
Tomlin, Lily 228
Townsend, Robert 21, 46,
    65
Tripp, Juan 10
Trout, Jack 24, 42, 117, 151,
    152, 199
Truman, Harry S. 76
Trump, Donald 162

Tucker, Malcolm 189
"Tuld, John" 69
Turgot, Anne Robert 208
Turner, Robert 8
Turner, Ted 8, 80
Twain, Mark 123

Van der Veer, Jeroen 123
Van Gogh, Vincent 15,
    103
Veblen, Thorstein 28
Veen, Jeffrey 67
Vermeulen, Freek 42, 43
Vonnegut, Karl 213

Walton, Sam 8, 59–60
Wanamaker, John 6
Wang, Vera 125
Ward, Artemus 159
Warhol, Andy 14, 15
Washington, Booker T.
    164
Watkins, Bill 22, 119
Waugh, Auberon 218
Weber, Max 25
Welch, Jack 22, 25, 36,
    199–200, 228
Welles, Orson 93

Wells, H.G. 6
Western Union 175
White, Slappy 216
Whyte, William 25, 53,
    213–14
Wildavsky, Ben 76
Wilde, Oscar 21, 36, 60,
    74, 130, 135, 153, 166,
    214
Wilson, Earl 203
Wilson, Woodrow 54,
    209, 210
Winters, Jonathan 203
Wired magazine 92
Wittgenstein, Ludwig 172
Woolman, C.E. 10
Wouk, Herman 208
Wrigley, William 65
Wyse, Lois 229

Xun Zi 9

Young, Andrew 132

Zappa, Frank 26, 161
Ziglar, Zig 214
Zymen, Sergio 24, 148,
    151, 193